GM.147

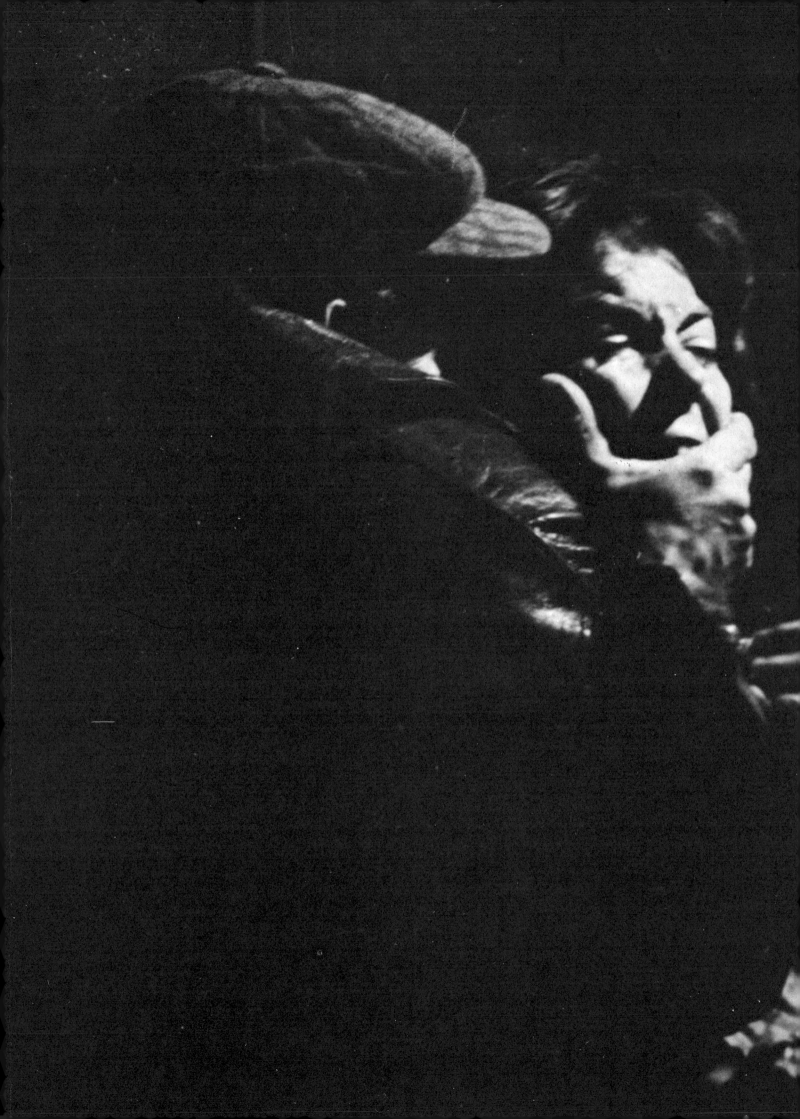

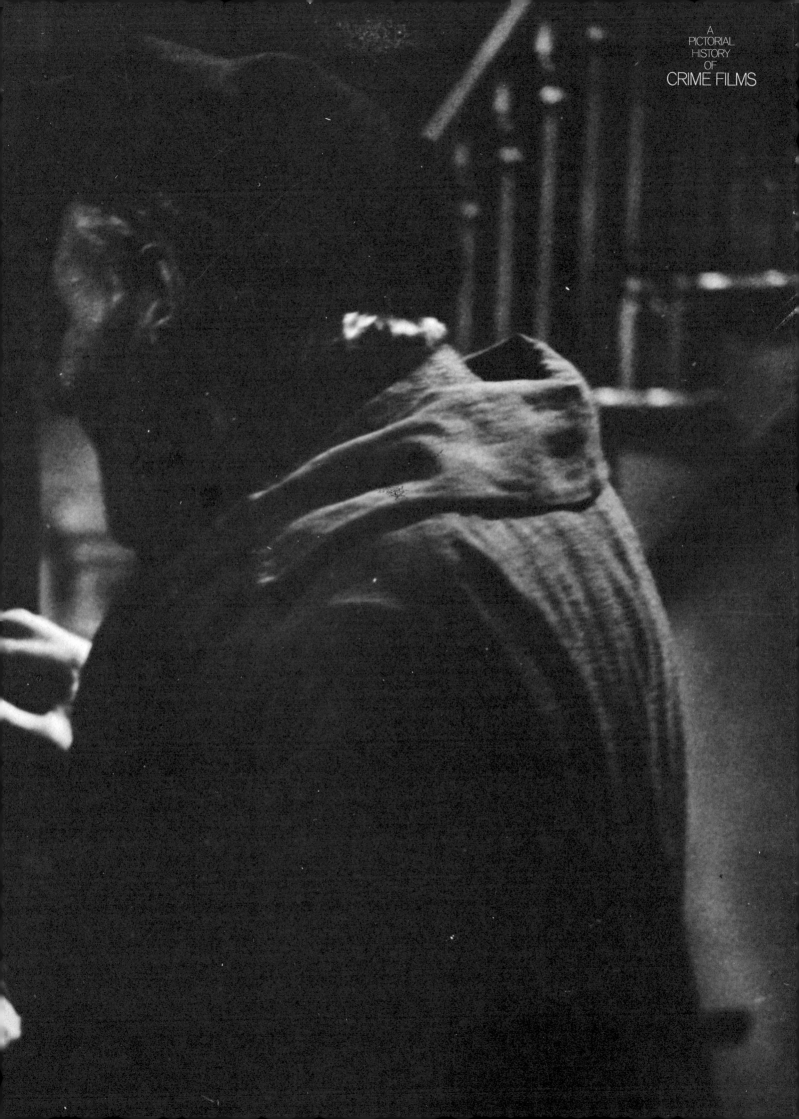

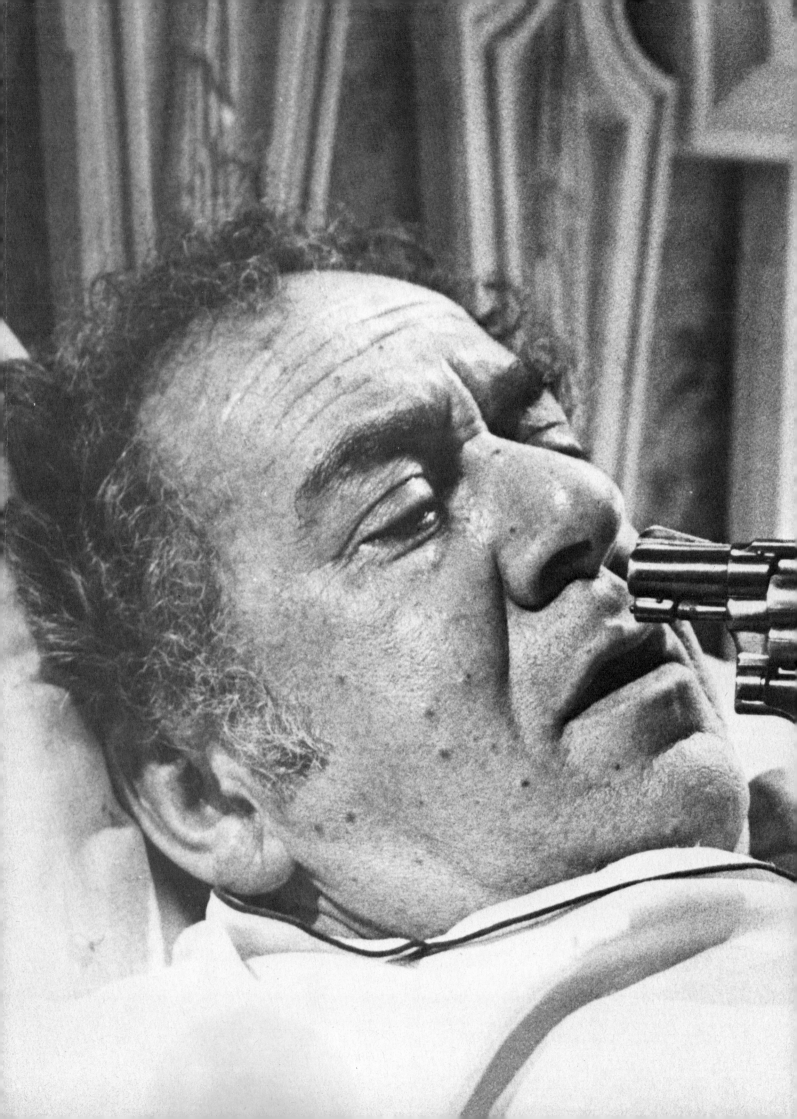

IAN CAMERON

A PICTORIAL HISTORY OF

CRIME

FILMS

HAMLYN

LONDON NEW YORK SYDNEY TORONTO

The photographs on the endpapers
and preliminary pages are as follows:
endpapers:
James Cagney in *'G' Men.*
half-title page:
Zohra Lampert being terrorised in *Pay or Die.*
title page:
Larry Haines and Roy Scheider in *The Seven Ups.*
this page:
George C. Scott and Stacy Keach in
The New Centurions.

Published by The Hamlyn Publishing Group Limited   London · New York · Sydney · Toronto
Astronaut House, Feltham, Middlesex, England

Copyright © The Hamlyn Publishing Group Limited 1975
ISBN 0 600 37022 4
Printed in England by Jarrold and Sons Limited, Norwich

CONTENTS

By rooting among the surviving artefacts of cinematic archaeology, one could doubtless nominate some one-reel epic as the very first crime movie. It might, for instance, be Edwin S. Porter's *The Great Train Robbery* of 1903, although this has as much claim to the position of ancestral western. Even the British cinema was producing crime movies in the first decade of this century, including the various versions of *The Life of Charles Peace*, the film biography of a celebrated villain from the then recent past.

However, the crime movie as a genre is a much later development. There seems little point in trying to trace the portrayal of crime through the silent cinema – in any case a purely scholarly exercise which would have to depend to a large extent on unverifiable descriptions of long-vanished pictures. Most of the evidence has disappeared. But at least in the early part of the silent period, the environment in which crime movies could become established as a genre had not yet developed.

One can detect historical forces at work in all manner of ways shaping the output of the film industry, obviously as in the wave of patriotic war movies produced during the Second World War, or more subtly as in the political under-currents that run through the post-war west-ern. But no genre has been more consistently shaped by factors from outside the cinema than the crime movie. It demands to be seen in the context of actual crime and constantly refers to identifiable people, events or situations, an aspect which it would be perverse of the film critic to ignore.

What paved the way for crime movies, or rather for their central form, gangster movies, was the change in the public image of American

Previous page: Josef Von Sternberg's *Underworld.*
Opposite: Lana Turner and Richard Basehart in Michael Gordon's *Portrait in Black.*

George Bancroft as 'Bull' Weed and Evelyn Brent as 'Feathers' McCoy in *Underworld*.

Right: Humphrey Bogart in his first major screen part, a role which he had previously taken on Broadway, Duke Mantee in Archie Mayo's *The Petrified Forest* (1936).

crime after the end of the First World War. Lawlessness was, of course, nothing new in the United States: in the west, organised gangs like that of the James brothers were operating in the reconstruction period after the Civil War. And in 1890, Police Chief Hennessey, investigating gang wars in the New Orleans docks, was assassinated by the Mafia. Nineteen Sicilians were tried and acquitted, but eleven of them were lynched by angry mobs.

Urban crime at the turn of the century was predominantly an ethnic matter, with predators and prey often coming from the same ghettoes. New York was the hunting ground of rival and often warring immigrant gangs; in the city's Chinatown, the great tong war of 1909 led to over fifty deaths. When the mayhem reached such spectacular proportions or became otherwise newsworthy, the public was inevitably outraged, as it was by the rise of the white slave trade, by Black Hand extortionists whose attentions extended to Caruso himself,

Standard gangster film imagery: *The Big Shot*.

and by the shooting of Owney 'The Killer' Madden, leader of a gang called The Gophers, in a New York dance hall in 1912. Not, however, until after the First World War did organised crime really start capturing the headlines. First of all, there were the operations of Arnold 'The Brain' Rothstein, who was behind the wholesale thefts of Liberty Bonds, for which he managed to manœuvre the blame on to a gambler called Jules W. Arndt Stein or Nicky Arnstein, the husband of Broadway star Fanny Brice. More spectacularly, Rothstein masterminded the fixing of the 1919 World Series.

But the land of opportunity did not become the promised land for organised crime until 16 January 1920, when the Volstead Act became law: '*Prohibition*. Manufacture, sale, transportation, importation, exportation, possession, etc., of intoxicating liquors prohibited . . .' In a country the size of the United States, Prohibition would have been unenforceable even by the most selflessly crusading of

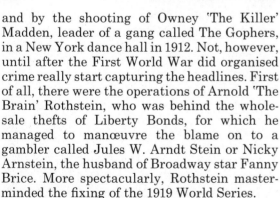

régimes. As the Director of New York's Bureau of Public Health Education wrote in 1923, '. . . the United States is bounded on the north by hard liquor, on the south by liquor, on the west by rum and on the east by no limit. . . . Those wanting a drink will get it, law or no law. The man too lazy to attend church just around the corner will walk five miles to keep a date with his bootlegger.' A vast number of citizens saw little reason to respect the Volstead Law, and as catering to their thirst was a crime, the criminals could see the whole nation as their clientele.

Out of the enormous profits, there was plenty of cash available for bribing police and politicians. From 1921, the remarkably corrupt Harding administration was in power; the President had his own official bootlegger and everyone seemed to be on the take, from the Attorney-General downwards. The gangsters had achieved a new status, capturing the attention and the imagination of the public. They had become incredibly wealthy – by 1927, Al Capone's net profits were estimated to be at least $60,000,000 a year. Many gangsters lived flamboyantly and spent lavishly. Even their funerals were of unparalleled splendour. Here apparently was a new breed of robber baron, whose violence was a matter of record, with gangland killings splattered across the front pages of the country's newspapers. Equipped with his own demonic allure and a steady blaze of free publicity, the gangster had become the perfect protagonist for a movie.

Before falling out, Ben Hecht and Josef von Sternberg agreed that in *Underworld* they made the first film built round a gangster. In his autobiography, 'Fun in a Chinese Laundry', Sternberg wrote: 'I was handed a few leaves of a scribbled manuscript written by Ben Hecht, his initial attempt to show his contempt for the "movies". It had a good title and dealt with the escapades of a gangster. It was untried material, as no films had as yet been made of this deplorable phase of our culture.' Sternberg completed the film in four weeks without any major stars. 'Without the benefit of the tush and gush of normal publicity which heralds every film as the greatest ever produced, my film opened at ten in the morning to avoid a

Angie Dickinson and Ronald Reagan in Don Siegel's 1964 version of *The Killers*.

review by the press, no critic being awake that early. Three hours later, Times Square was blocked by a huge crowd seeking to gain admission to the theatre, a crowd that stayed there and forced the theatre to stay open all night and remain open all night for the balance of the long run, thus inaugurating the era of gangster films and exhibitions of films around the clock.' Even allowing for Sternberg's characteristic lack of modesty, the success of *Underworld* was clearly sufficient to encourage others to make gangster movies. While it would be rash to describe *Underworld* as the first gangster movie – there was a feature called *The Bootleggers* copyrighted in 1922, and Lewis Milestone filmed a play called *The Racket* in 1928 – Sternberg's film was effectively the beginning of the genre as it was the first gangster movie to make a big impression on the public.

It was made two years after Al Capone inherited power in Chicago (or rather control of about a quarter of the city) from Johnny Torrio. *Underworld* was released on 29 October 1927. Less than six months later came the event which, more than any other, became the symbol of underworld violence. The St Valentine's Day

Massacre was not a complete success as it did not include its prime target, George 'Bugs' Moran, but the wiping out of seven Moran associates helped build up the Capone image. 'Only the Capone gang kills like that', said Moran. The year 1928, however, brought a very much more momentous happening: the stock market crash of 29 October marked the beginning of the Depression. The only people around having a good time were the hoods – their activities were the one facet of contemporary American life endowed with excitement. And however much films set out to expose the evils of gangland, audiences would also get to share vicariously in its unprincipled pleasures.

Underworld, a silent picture, opened on Broadway in the same month as *The Jazz Singer*. Dialogue turned out to be as important to the crime film as it was to another genre which developed in the 'thirties, the screwball comedy. The dialogue gave crime movies much of their flavour, starting with the steely terseness of the opening speeches by Edward G. Robinson in *Little Caesar*: 'Diamond Pete Montana – he doesn't have to waste his time on cheap gas stations. He's somebody. He's in the big time, doing things in a big way. And look at

16

us – just a couple of nobodies. Nothing. . . . Say, I could do all the things that fellow does, and more, only I never got my chance. . . . What is there to be afraid of? And when I get in a tight corner, I'll shoot my way out of it. Why, sure. Sure. Shoot first and argue afterwards. . . .'

This book, then, concentrates on American crime movies of the sound era. The form it takes is shaped by two problems which confront anyone who tries to write about a film genre: the availability of the films and the difficulty of defining the genre.

Unlike old books, old movies are not readily available for inspection; the Byzantine complexities of the film business mean that even the acknowledged classics are frequently vault-bound. Crime movies include only a tiny proportion of acknowledged classics. Their continuity and development takes in a vast mass of pictures making up a genre which is a sort of critical iceberg, most of it submerged among the B-features and other low-budget pictures which would hardly have been mentioned in the press outside the columns of the trade papers. In any case, secondhand reports are virtually useless – relying largely on their memories, critics are likely to disagree about what has happened in a film, let alone about how to interpret it. As far as possible, I shall discuss only those films I have seen quite recently, using factual quotes to cover some others. But as far as film criticism is concerned, a great proportion of the movies which should be taken into account have retreated into obscurity, leaving little more behind them than a copyright record. Mere lists of titles suggest developments which a diligent researcher could follow up: 1938 produced a good crop of prison movies, while that and the following year also seemed to offer an unusual number of gangster films, perhaps in

the wake of the Big Heat which had started in the middle of 1937 when Louis 'Lepke' Buchalter, head of what was later to be known as Murder Inc., went on the lam and ended shortly after 10 pm on 24 August 1939 when Buchalter, with the help of Walter Winchell, then the syndicated columnist of the New York 'Daily Mirror', surrendered to J. Edgar Hoover. The films may have been made in the wake of the publicity attending the Big Heat, but effectively they survive only as a string of evocative titles: *Extortion, Law of the Underworld, Gangs of New York, Smashing the Rackets* and so on. Any attempt at a conventional history of crime movies in the circumstances would be stretched to breaking-point between the occasional peaks of viewability.

The problem of definition comes up increasingly as one tries to examine the genre as such: what exactly is a crime movie? In common with almost every other genre, it seems to exist less and less as a definable group the more one looks at it. Clearly *Little Caesar* and the other gangster movies have to be included, but so do police movies and private-eye movies which are obviously concerned with crimes. So far, so simple: but plenty of other movies are concerned with crime and could equally be claimed by some other genre. Richard Fleischer's *Violent Saturday*, which was written by the ingenious Sidney Boehm, exemplifies the intergeneric hybrid. As the story of three hoods robbing a bank, it is a crime movie, but it is equally concerned to take apart the society of its small-town setting and thus belongs, too, among such related sagas as *Some Came Running* and *Peyton Place*.

Of course, *Peyton Place* itself is not exactly devoid of crime, though of a cosily domestic variety – Arthur Kennedy tries to rape his step-

Ann Sheridan, Frank McHugh, James Cagney and Anthony Quinn in Anatole Litvak's *City for Conquest* (1940).

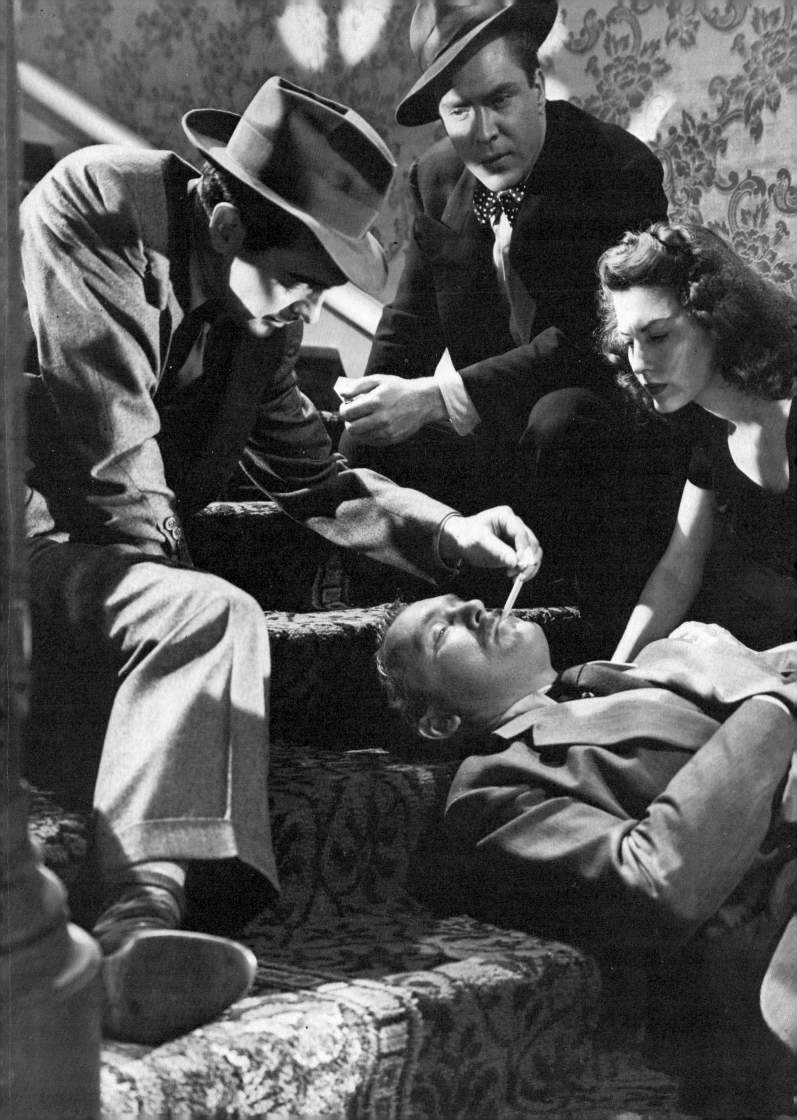

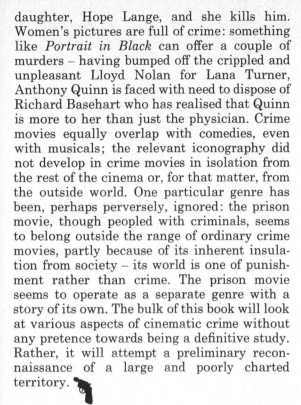

daughter, Hope Lange, and she kills him. Women's pictures are full of crime: something like *Portrait in Black* can offer a couple of murders – having bumped off the crippled and unpleasant Lloyd Nolan for Lana Turner, Anthony Quinn is faced with need to dispose of Richard Basehart who has realised that Quinn is more to her than just the physician. Crime movies equally overlap with comedies, even with musicals; the relevant iconography did not develop in crime movies in isolation from the rest of the cinema or, for that matter, from the outside world. One particular genre has been, perhaps perversely, ignored: the prison movie, though peopled with criminals, seems to belong outside the range of ordinary crime movies, partly because of its inherent insulation from society – its world is one of punishment rather than crime. The prison movie seems to operate as a separate genre with a story of its own. The bulk of this book will look at various aspects of cinematic crime without any pretence towards being a definitive study. Rather, it will attempt a preliminary reconnaissance of a large and poorly charted territory.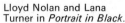

Left: Sam Levene, Edmond O'Brien, Ava Gardner and Albert Dekker in Robert Siodmak's 1946 version of *The Killers*.

Lloyd Nolan and Lana Turner in *Portrait in Black*.

19

No other genre overlaps with the crime movie to the same extent as the thriller. There are, however, plenty of thrillers which do not contain any elements of crime, particularly stories of escape or rescue, and there are crime movies which could not in any way be described as thrillers, that is to say films built around suspense. The whole business of suspense, though, is intimately concerned with the attitude of the audience to the characters on the screen, and its presence or absence is very relevant to the impact of crime movies.

Suspense might be defined as the heightening of the spectator's concern about the outcome of the action he is watching. It can be built up, at least on a moment-to-moment basis, independently of any characterisation, without any feeling for the protagonists as individuals. This purely physical suspense depends in large measure on feelings about the integrity of the human body; it is the suspense that attends some performance like tightrope-walking, where the penalty of failure is likely to be quite messy. The threat needs to be pretty extreme – unless it involves a character about whom we have some feelings, mere shooting or stabbing is not a possibility likely to unsettle us too much – we are sufficiently inured to such spectacles in the movies and, at least until recently, we could be reasonably sure that screen convention would prevent them being visually revolting. The sort of wincing apprehension that goes with purely physical suspense is mainly the stock-in-trade of the horror movie – for example, Edgar Allan Poe's *Pit and the Pendulum* image of the inexorably descending blade swinging back and forth above the exposed abdomen.

Previous page: Lee Remick and Ross Martin's feet in *An Experiment in Terror.*
Opposite: Tippi Hedren in the title part of *Marnie.*

22

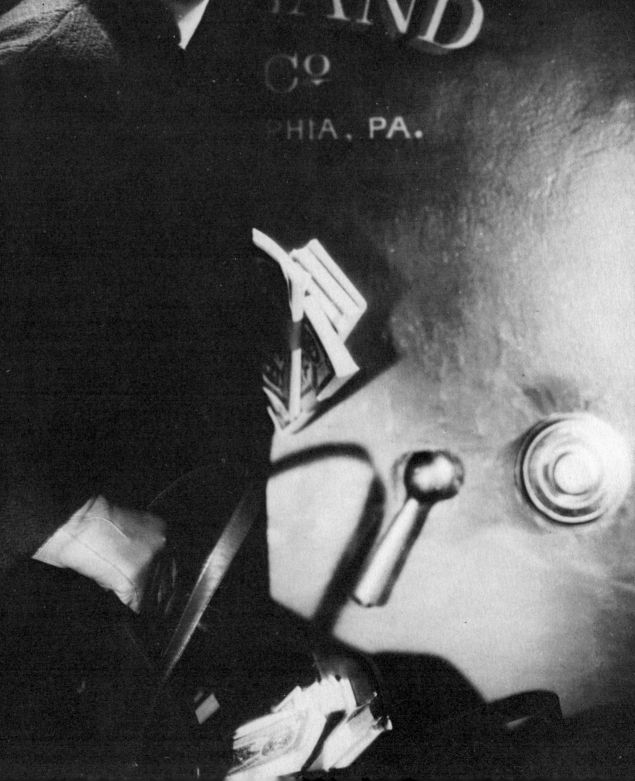

Two pieces of physical suspense. *Above:* Jack Palance and Robert Mitchum on a cable car in Rudolph Maté's 3-D film *Second Chance. Opposite:* George Kennedy and Cary Grant on the edge of a Parisian rooftop in Stanley Donen's *Charade* (1963).

Even in less specialised forms, physical elements are often deployed to increase the suspense. An extra measure of danger added to, say, a climatic fight will help make us forget that the Hays Code rules will ensure the defeat of the heavy. Thus the inexorable advance of a snowplough at just such a moment in Jacques Tourneur's *Nightfall* opens up the possibility that at least one of the combatants will get minced. The film-maker is able to unsettle the audience by playing on its fears, and by all manner of other techniques that amount to psychological manipulation of the spectators.

The great movie for this sort of manipulation is Blake Edwards's *An Experiment in Terror* (retitled *The Grip of Fear* for British consumption after it had failed to appeal to the female audience in America). To increase our disquiet, the film is filled with images of precariousness – sometimes the camera cranes upwards although it is already at the top of a hill; there are also shots looking down from a helicopter tracking cars along a road. The precarious images start as early as the second and fourth shots of the film, under the credit titles, accompanied by Henry Mancini's eerie music (which is played with such spooky slowness that the recorded version is taken at a quicker tempo). The second shot looks straight down on the approach to the Golden Gate Bridge as a pale-coloured convertible shoots into the frame; the camera tilts up as the car drives away. The fourth shot looks out over the bonnet of the car and pans round on to the heroine driving. To produce a close shot of her, the camera field is narrowed with a zoom-in; the fast forward motion of the car and the illusion of slow movement in the opposite direction by the camera as the bonnet gradually disappears from the bottom of the frame combine to give a curious and uniquely unsettling sensation of slipping off the front of the car. Blake Edwards is able to extract a threatening quality from things that are in themselves perfectly harmless: a big close-up of the rear light of the heroine's car appears particularly sinister. In the opening sequence of *An Experiment in Terror*, Edwards also uses more predictable audience reactions like fear of the dark and feeling for a young girl menaced by a psychopath. Later, he also uses shock cuts from one sequence to the next.

These techniques are designed to increase our disquiet and thus to accentuate the suspense. They would be useless or even actively irritating without a central focus for our concern, a character for whom we feel something on a personal level. There can be very little suspense in a film where we do not care what happens to the characters, and some burst of physical excitement like a car chase can do no more than provide an alternative of short duration.

The most effective foundation, then, for suspense is the audience's identification with one or more of the characters, an identification which seems to be a natural reaction to movies and is so strong that audiences are going to

Janet Leigh and Anthony
Perkins in *Psycho*.

Lee Remick in *An
Experiment in Terror*.

identify almost automatically with someone on
the screen, unless prevented from doing so, by
assorted alienation devices or by the simple un-
availability of any characters who are remotely
sympathetic or attractive.

Identification and suspense work together
cumulatively, for suspense tends to force us
into closer identification. Alfred Hitchcock
has always been the greatest manipulator of
this interaction, showing unparalleled dex-
terity in switching our identification around
between one character and another. Hitchcock
thrusts us into a position of complicity in theft
with Janet Leigh in *Psycho* and with Tippi
Hedren as the kleptomaniac heroine of *Marnie*
by having us on the edges of our seats in the fear
that they will be caught. In *Psycho* we also have
a moment of identification with Anthony
Perkins in his disposal of Janet Leigh's body –
as he watches her car, containing her corpse
wrapped in the shower curtain, sink into a
swamp, it stops with a good part of it still exposed, and there are a few moments when we
share his worry before the car resumes its
sinking and disappears from sight.

If suspense can be used to put us emotionally
on the side of characters who are in the act of
breaking the law, its arrival in a crime movie
becomes pretty important. The popular cinema
relies very little on detached contemplation.
The real progress of a movie is summed up less
by a deadpan summary of the action than by
analysis of the way audience reaction develops
during its course. Here lies another problem for
the film critic: apart from sometimes being very
difficult to describe accurately and honestly,
reactions are not constant and universal but
are modified by the personality of each spec-

tator, even by his awareness – it would hardly
be possible today to view films from, say, Nazi
Germany or Cold War Hollywood without
being influenced by a strong dose of hindsight
about their less savoury implications.

There is one variety of crime movie which is
almost devoid of suspense: the classic gangster
picture of the early 'thirties and its pastiche
historical descendants which appeared around
1960, films like *The Rise and Fall of Legs Diamond*. In the first cycle, one discouragement to
identification was the choice of actors. Possibly
in acknowledgment of the unloveliness of the
real archetypes, the leading gangsters were
often cast with such physically unprepossessing figures as Edward G. Robinson, James
Cagney and Paul Muni (though Cagney in particular did compensate with an overdose of
pugnacious energy).

The year 1930, when *Little Caesar* was made,
also saw the application of the Hays Code. This
set of rules was designed to ensure that Hollywood's products would never offend anyone, at
least anyone who could make trouble and possibly therefore threaten profits. For thirty
years, the Code formed the limits within which
film-makers had to work. Apart from conceal-
ing the embarrassing existence of the human
navel and protecting the public from such rude
words as 'damn' or 'nuts' and from displays of
lewd and lascivious dancing, the Code was particularly strong on the matter of crime and
punishment: no infringement of the law was
ever to go unpunished in a movie. Despite clear
evidence that many real villains were still
doing very nicely, gangsters in Hollywood
movies were almost invariably doomed.

The conjunction of these inescapable rules

with characters who were unexciting in appearance and ugly in deed produced a spectacle which was the very opposite of suspense. The gangster's preordained destruction has a strong element of ritual about it. Instead of suspense, the audience is presented with an edifying display of just deserts. In the 1960 gangster cycle, relaxation of Code restrictions and nostalgic distance from the events depicted allowed for more overt enjoyment of the subject's rise to power and even some better-looking heroes. But the merciless final destruction remains, and it is notable in *The Rise and Fall of Legs Diamond* how the audience is turned against the initially likeable Diamond – he is destroyed for us before he is actually killed.

Gangster biographies have inherently very little suspense, but it is possible to present almost any story in a way which removes the suspense which it might contain. Without looking into the very personal methods of Jean-Luc Godard's crime movies such as *Breathless* and *Pierrot le Fou*, one can find a very striking example in a Hollywood film of the 'thirties, Fritz Lang's *You Only Live Once*.

Henry Fonda emerges from his third stretch in prison to go to a new job found for him by the Public Defender whose secretary (Sylvia Sidney) he marries. He cannot escape the stigma of his record: he loses his job and is convicted and sentenced to death for a bank robbery in which he had no part. On the night set for his execution, he escapes, killing the Prison Chaplain who is trying to make him believe that he has just been cleared (the truth). His wife goes on the run with him, but they are both shot by the police before they can get across the border.

Lang could scarcely show less interest in any

excitement which might be found in this story. His theme is the man's inability to avoid his cruel fate. To this end, Lang repeatedly undercuts any question about the possible outcome of a sequence by showing us in advance some very clear indication of what is going to happen. Even the brief idyll of the wedding night includes a cut away to the hotel proprietor remembering Fonda's face and starting to flip through the real-life crime magazines of which he just happens to be an avid reader. The result of this treatment is that by the time Fonda does anything potentially exciting like trying to break out of jail the odds are so clearly rigged against him that we simply assume that everything else is going to go wrong. The extent to which the world is against Fonda in the first few reels of the film is sufficient to undermine the credibility of the film; Lang himself, talking about it almost thirty years after it was made, opined that it was a little 'constructed'.

In other hands, the same story might have been played for suspense, at least in part, as sympathetic characters in an ambiguous or definitely guilty position in the eyes of the law can be very powerful identification figures for suspense. The legally ambiguous characters are particularly valuable in crime thrillers as we cannot rely on the comfort of a final verdict that is clearly predictable with the help of the Hays Code. A thriller, incidentally, is no more than a film in which suspense plays a dominant part – there are plenty of films containing suspenseful sequences which cannot as a whole be taken as thrillers. Thus *Roadhouse*, for example, is a fair specimen of 'forties triangle drama until its last sequence in which Richard Widmark, unhinged by the loss of Ida Lupino

Left and above: Ray Danton as Legs Diamond in *The Rise and Fall of Legs Diamond*. Holding the dance competition trophy he has won for them by unfair means is Karen Steele.

The ending of *Scarface* with police and (*right*) Paul Muni as Tony Camonte.

to Cornel Wilde, hunts the couple in the woods at night with murderous intent.

The thriller can be looked at first of all as a mechanism. Its primary aim is to keep us thrilled for the best part of an hour and a half, a task which has to be tackled in the light of certain basic principles. Perhaps the most important of these is that the movie audience is a lot more sophisticated than it was in the days of silent cliff-hangers. It has grown resistant to suspense because its knowledge of the well-established rules has made it blasé. At least until the early 'sixties when the rules started to break down, audiences were unlikely to be automatically excited by the question of whether the hero would arrive in time to save the heroine from a fate worse than death at the hands of the heavy (though in the 'seventies such a question might regain some of its suspense as there would be every chance of her getting thoroughly raped before the appearance of her rescuer). Suspense no longer comes easily; the director has to work quite astutely to achieve it.

With the spectator sitting smugly in his seat, in effect challenging the director to thrill him, there is no chance of suspense unless his feelings of security are demolished. After all, he is sure that the good guy will emerge triumphant in time for the end title, while whatever remains of the heavy will probably be destined for the morgue. So why should he get worked up on the hero's behalf? The director's aim must therefore be to make the customers forget that they know the ending; they must be so ensnared by the movie that their feelings are entirely taken up with what will happen next rather than with what will happen eventually.

This state can be achieved by sudden shock

therapy as in *An Experiment in Terror*, which then supports its suspense with an orchestration of disturbing visual effects. We are in a state of suspense within a minute of the credit titles ending: Kelly Sherwood (Lee Remick) has driven home at night to the quiet Twin Peaks suburb of San Francisco. As she gets out of the car in her garage, a dog barks in the house. She mutters 'Oh, shut up, Murphy.' Then without any warning, the garage door swings down behind her. 'Is someone there?' she asks nervously. From somewhere very close comes the sound of heavy asthmatic breathing. Kelly moves around uncertainly in the darkness, and the camera follows closely. Suddenly a hand is thrust across her mouth, and she is held tightly from behind so that she is powerless to struggle. A breathless, grating voice says 'I'm not going to hurt you. No, no, no, I don't want to hurt *you*,' but the tone suggests that there are other things he does want to do. 'I've already killed twice, so I won't hesitate to do it again.' When the scarcely visible assailant takes his hand away from her mouth, Kelly gasps, 'What do you want?' 'You.' 'I'll scream.' This is a dead-end street.' 'You won't scream and I know what sort of a street this is.' He warns her not to do anything foolish. 'You'd be dead and I'd be out a hundred thousand dollars.'

Here the unexpected and apparently arbitrary menace is a sufficiently shattering realisation of commonplace fears to have us identifying immediately with a girl about whom we know nothing. Blake Edwards uses frontal attack to get us unreservedly involved in his heroine's predicament. The same position can be reached gradually and by stealth as in Alfred Hitchcock's second version of *The Man Who Knew Too Much* (a much richer and more complex

28

piece of work than the 'thirties original). In the relaxed opening sequences, we get to know and like Ben McKenna (James Stewart), his wife Jo (Doris Day), and their son Hank (Christopher Olsen) who are on holiday in North Africa. We share a little of their boredom: on the bus from Casablanca to Marrakesh, Jo complains that they saw the same scenery on the way to Las Vegas the previous summer. Then we are caught up in her curiosity about a helpful and charming Frenchman, Louis Bernard (Daniel Gelin) who evades all questions about himself while seeming to Jo, and us, to be trying to find out all about them. From curiosity, we move to suspicion that they are being watched – we have not yet learned the one piece of information that would make it perfectly natural for people to stare at Jo (she was a big star of Broadway musicals until her retirement only a year or two before).

Cocktails with Bernard are interrupted by a knock on the door of their hotel suite. Now Hitchcock administers our first shock – not a big one but enough to make us slightly uneasy. At the door is a sinister-looking individual. As the camera tracks quickly into a close-up of him, his face is suddenly illuminated – after opening the door to him, Jo (offscreen) switches on the light. We notice that the man is not looking at Jo but straight into the distance where we know Bernard is standing. Jo's (and our) suspicions are confirmed after the visitor has gone away with the excuse that he knocked on the wrong door: Bernard makes a telephone call in incomprehensibly muttered French, then remembers 'an important matter' that will stop him taking dinner with them.

Hitchcock's carefully laid preparations for the suspense are complete but for an apparent reversal in the build-up of unease which will have devastating effects later. In a restaurant, the middle-aged couple who have been staring at the McKennas before engage them in conversation and turn out to be reassuringly affable. The Draytons (Bernard Miles and Brenda de Banzie), unlike Bernard, are only too willing to talk about themselves: 'Edward was a big noise in the Ministry of Food during the war.' Now he is in Marrakesh for 'these United Nations fellas'. The Draytons may be pretty boring but at least they are clearly harmless. The picture of the Draytons as security personified is reinforced by the arrival of Bernard with a girl. The restaurant scene ends on these two sitting behind an open-work screen (which makes them look suspicious). They speak in French, but it does not take a linguist to make out what they are talking about. 'Is that the couple you're looking for?' says the girl. 'Yes, that's them.' Hitchcock often uses the fade-out at the end of a scene, as here, to fix an impression in the mind of the spectator. What, of course, we do not know is that the couple being discussed is not the McKennas but the Draytons.

Having prepared the ground thoroughly, Hitchcock is ready to start the action. A visit to the market-place is interrupted when Hank sees an Arab being chased by another who in turn is chased by the police. Mrs Drayton restrains Hank from running after them: 'It's best to keep out of trouble, Hank.' A few moments later, the first Arab, who is really Bernard in disguise, staggers towards them with a knife in his back and collapses into Ben's arms.

'Out of five thousand people in the Great Market Place, why does he choose you when he is about to die?' The Police Inspector is only echoing a question that Ben has already asked himself. Hitchcock's heroes are usually entitled to ask themselves 'Why me?' Farley Granger's selection by the murderously inclined Robert Walker to exchange victims in *Strangers on a Train* and Cary Grant's kidnapping by James Mason's henchmen at the beginning of *North by Northwest* suddenly interrupt pleasant and prosperous existences to plunge the two heroes into situations in which their very survival is at stake.

In the Hitchcock world, anything can become

Shooting the last scene of *Scarface*.

29

Anna Karina and Jean-Paul Belmondo in *Pierrot le fou*.

dangerous at any time: in *The Man Who Knew Too Much*, it is the kindly Mrs Drayton who volunteers to take Hank back to the hotel while his parents are being questioned by the police after Louis Bernard's death, but she actually kidnaps him. People can be trapped in agonising and even fatal situations by pure chance: Marion Crane (Janet Leigh) arrives at the Bates Motel in *Psycho* because she has lost her way and driven off the main highway by mistake in a blinding rainstorm. But who sent the rain? Clearly the same fellow who brought the almost Biblical plague of *The Birds* on the inhabitants of Bodega Bay. In the movies, the director can have the role of God. Hitchcock is perhaps the only director to take the part wholeheartedly. He is the manipulator of coincidence: it is he who involves the McKenna family in a political assassination in London by making a bus from Casablanca to Marrakesh swerve on the road (Hank's accidental removal of an Arab woman's veil introduces them to Louis Bernard who helps sort out the ensuing argument). Hitchcock's aim is that the audience shall be as much in his power emotionally as the characters are physically.

One of the many reasons for Hitchcock being by far the greatest exponent of the film thriller is the unique degree of compatibility between his vision and the mechanics of his chosen medium of expression. Hitchcock's world, full of uncertainties, of potential and

Sylvia Sidney and Henry Fonda in *You Only Live Once*.

Richard Widmark and Cornel Wilde in *Roadhouse*.

actual hazards, is an intensification of the view of things that any thriller needs to elicit from its audience. The lack of succour available to the hero from the people and objects around him can take on a thematic weight in Hitchcock movies.

Isolation in a hostile world is one of the key thriller situations. Even with the entire San Francisco police force on her side, Lee Remick as Kelly in *An Experiment in Terror* is effectively alone as she cannot get in touch with the police for fear that the evil Red Lynch will find out. She has to go through the whole process of stealing $100,000 from the bank where she works exactly as he has told her. The lack of contact between Kelly and the police or Kelly and Red Lynch (who mainly makes his presence felt by telephone) gives *An Experiment in Terror* much of its chilling quality. The London sequences of *The Man Who Knew Too Much* are treated in a rather similar way. This is Hitchcock's telephone movie: fifteen calls are made, or about to be made, when a character is interrupted. These calls have the function of allowing the plot to proceed while the characters are far apart. The separation of Ben and Jo for much of the time after they get to London removes a possible source of comfort for them. Their isolation from both police and heavies also removes the reassuring chance of doing something – when the opponent is within reach, there is always the happy possibility of a solution through violence. Until there can be some sort of confrontation, the conclusion is delayed, and delay – drawing out the agony – is the very basis of suspense. 'A suspense story is not simply a Who-done-it,' wrote Hitchcock in his preface to 'My Favourites in Suspense'. 'It might better be called a When's-he-gonna-do-it.'

Suspense can be built towards events we desire or events we fear, or can be balanced between the two – robbery sequences, for instance, can elicit in the audience desire for success coupled with fear of interruption. In any case, a director of any skill can build up our feelings by withholding the outcome for as long as possible. The main climax of *The Man Who Knew Too Much* is a fantastic piece of virtuosity in this respect, lasting 124 shots, twelve minutes without any dialogue. We know that a visiting statesman is to be assassinated at a gala concert in the Royal Albert Hall. The shot will coincide with the crash of cymbals in Arthur Benjamin's 'Storm Cloud Cantata'; only Jo McKenna knows that there is anything amiss, and her son is being held by the assassin's colleagues. We know that nothing can happen to the statesman until the crucial moment in the music. 'Listen for the crash of the cymbals', said Mr Drayton as he played the record to the gunman. We think we know when the crash will come as we have already heard it four times. The first, an hour and a half previously, was in an abridged orchestral version played behind the credit titles. The other three were very short extracts played on a portable gramophone – we heard the crash but almost nothing preceding it. So, in fact, we don't know but think we do. The music provides any number of opportunities for a cymbal crash. The result is that we keep thinking: it's going to happen now. The repeated denial of our expectations is just one element in the sequence's elaborate pattern of delay and frustration: suspense is not a matter of speeding things up towards the climax, as we would like, but of slowing them down.

Planning a suspense film is very much a matter of strategy, of manœuvring the story components to produce the required effect on the audience. Such tactical details as the order in which information is presented can shape the film's impact – thus the temporary withholding of the news that Jo McKenna was a Broadway star increases our disquiet early in *The Man Who Knew Too Much*. There is a whole range of ploys that can be classified as red herrings, an extremely variable species that includes false leads, people or facts not as suspicious as they seem, and suspense sequences that lead nowhere. Hitchcock has harnessed the red herring to express his picture of a capricious, deceptive, threatening world – shoals of them can be observed performing assorted functions in his movies. At the simplest, there is the apparently suspicious motorcycle cop whose presence scares Janet Leigh when she is absconding with the money in *Psycho*. In *The Man Who Knew Too Much*, a more straightforward thriller, an elaborate red herring has Ben McKenna setting on an innocent taxidermist called Ambrose Chappell in Camden Town when he should be at the Nonconformist Ambrose Chapel in Bayswater, the cover under which the Draytons run their

assassination squad. In the same film, the treatment of Mrs Drayton is a whole series of deceptions: her image is first implanted in our minds as suspicious loiterer, then elaborately defused into harmless stick-in-the-mud before she is revealed as politically motivated kidnapper. In a final reversal, she becomes kind and self-sacrificing.

It takes strategic planning, too, to sustain the suspense right through the film, particularly as the final outcome will be governed by the Hays Code certainties, and the rest of the action will recognise that it is sound economics to keep the biggest (and thus most expensive) stars going until the last reel. This usually reliable principle was spectacularly shattered

Sylvia Sidney and Henry Fonda in *You Only Live Once*.

Leslie Banks, Nova Pilbeam and Peter Lorre in the 1934 version of *The Man Who Knew Too Much*.

James Stewart wrestling with a red herring in the 1956 version of *The Man Who Knew Too Much*.

Cary Grant finds himself in a compromising situation with Philip Ober in the United Nations building in Alfred Hitchcock's *North by Northwest* (1959).

in *Psycho* where Hitchcock polishes off his biggest star less than half-way through the film. But usually the rules do apply, and the planning has to take the audience's sophistication into account. Thus suspense can often be built up as subsidiary blocks of action which relate more or less obliquely to the final outcome – in *Strangers on a Train*, a suspense sequence is built round Robert Walker's efforts to retrieve Farley Granger's cigarette-lighter which he has accidentally dropped down a drain and which he is aiming to plant at the spot where he murdered Granger's wife.

One recurrent feature of post-war crime thrillers is obviously linked to the anti-suspense character of the Code. From Robert Siodmak's *The Killers* (1946) to Peter Yates's *The Friends of Eddie Coyle* (1973), robberies which form big suspense set-pieces are placed at the beginning of the film where they can be carried through to completion successfully – Nemesis can be postponed to the end of the movie, which is informed by a different sort of tension. Many movies about criminals derive their power largely from the inexorability of the rules. However sympathetically we may feel towards Humphrey Bogart in Raoul Walsh's *High Sierra* or Sterling Hayden in Stanley Kubrick's *The Killing*, we know that there cannot be a happy ending for either of them. The feelings we have developed towards these criminals makes their death or defeat a very different matter for us to the ritual destruction of Little Caesar Bandello or Legs Diamond. Movies about criminals were among the very few forms of tragedy available within the genres used by Hollywood in its post-war heyday.

The Code operated in a negative way: it was less concerned to see virtue rewarded than to make sure that infringements of its provisions were punished. On the whole, the rules were applied with total inflexibility, for instance to the Joan Bennett character in Fritz Lang's wartime picture *Manhunt*. Lang recalled to Peter Bogdanovich: '. . . naturally, the Hays Office insisted that we couldn't show or glamourize a prostitute – that's impossible.

(They said she should not swing her purse back and forth.) You know how we overcame it? We had to prominently show a sewing-machine in her apartment: thus she was not a whore, she was a "seamstress"!' The inflexibility actually allowed quite a lot of room for manœuvre. Undepictable sexual activity could always be indicated with a sly fade-out, a convention which came so well established that the scriptwriter Ben Hecht believed it was a widespread belief that whenever a movie scene faded out, the characters 'fell to futtering'. In crime movies, wrong could be done with great relish (within the limits, of course, of what could be shown or suggested) providing that the last reel held come-uppance for the transgressors. Just occasionally, the spirit of the Code rather than the letter was applied. In Lang's *Scarlet Street*, a 1945 remake of Jean Renoir's *La Chienne* (1931), Edward G. Robinson stabs his mistress (Joan Bennett) with an ice-pick, lets her boy friend Dan Duryea go to the electric chair for the murder, and survives the end title in liberty. Not that he goes completely unpunished: at the end, his paintings signed by her have been recognised as works of genius. In Lang's words: 'He sleeps on a bench in Central Park, he's cold; a policeman comes and hits him on the sole of his shoe. And he is an old man, unshaven, his mind still going around Joan Bennett whom he killed, whom he really loved and can't forget. He goes down a street and you hear "Jingle Bells, Jingle Bells . . .", everybody is happy. And out of an art gallery comes his last picture – the portrait he painted of her – and someone says "It's a very low price, only so-and-so many thousand dollars." And here is this bum who made it, and nobody knows it, and he goes away down the street, with her voice ringing in his ears.' The punishment, though not provided by the law, is there, much more than it ever was in Renoir's version, and Lang, knowing that there were Jesuits, who would appreciate this form of punishment, behind the Hays Office, never had the slightest difficulty with censorship on the film.

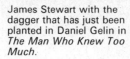
James Stewart with the dagger that has just been planted in Daniel Gelin in *The Man Who Knew Too Much*.

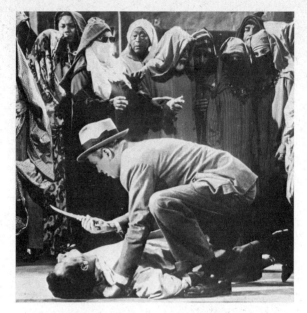

Scarlet Street shows just how far Hollywood movies could depart from what hostile critics see as an endless stream of mindlessly stereotyped happy endings. One might explain it away as a freak made possible by the combination of a determined director with an intelligent writer (Dudley Nichols) and a sympathetic producer (Walter Wanger) who was also the husband of one of the stars. But an even more unorthodox movie, which appeared in the following year, had none of these privileges but took the crime thriller about as far away from the convention of the happy ending as it is possible to get.

Edgar G. Ulmer's *Detour* was made for a short-lived Poverty Row outfit called PRC (Producer's Releasing Corporation), and is well in the running to be the cheapest really good talkie to come out of Hollywood. Most of it involves just three actors and a car in front of a back-projection machine. The two stars were Tom Neal, who was last heard of in the late 'sixties on a murder charge and described as 'landscape-gardener to the stars', and an extraordinary lady called Ann Savage, who looks like a younger Judith Anderson but with eyes which seem fit to turn people to stone.

Neal is hitchhiking across America to join his fiancée, an aspiring vocalist reduced to working as a hash-slinger in Los Angeles. He gets a lift from a loud-mouthed braggart who keeps taking pills and shows him his scars, some from a childhood wound with a sabre, some more recent and done by a female hitchhiker showing insufficient gratitude. The man, who's called Haskell, buys him dinner, then asks him to take the wheel for a bit while he sleeps. When our hero feels tired, he tries to wake his companion up, only to discover that Haskell is dead. He panics, and, relieving the dead man of his money and papers, dumps the body in a wood and drives on. He pulls up at a motel and has a troubled sleep.

Next morning, he's driving away when he sees a hitchhiker. 'Man,' he narrates, 'she looked like she got thrown off the crummiest freight train on earth.' This is Vera (Ann Savage). She goes straight off to sleep – 'The poor kid probably had had a rough time of it. . . . This nightmare was over.' He's feeling relieved when the poor kid opens her eyes and it quickly becomes apparent that all is not well – she was the hitchhiker who gave Haskell his scars. She recognises Haskell's car. 'I know a wrong guy when I see one. What did you do – kiss him with a wrench?' She is in no doubt that foul play has been involved. 'Remember, I knew Charlie Haskell better than you did.'

She blackmails him into selling the car, but before they can do so, they have to spend a night in a hotel suite in San Bernardino. She starts getting drunk and acting sexy – a prospect which is less than appetising to him as well as to us. 'Or is your conscience bothering you? So if it'll make you sociable you didn't kill him.' The car-selling plan is ditched by Vera when she reads in a paper that Haskell's rich father is at the point of death. Knowing that father and son have not met since Haskell was a child, she decides that a little impersonation should allow them to collect the inheritance. Another night in the hotel: they get drunk again. Vera, who has a mean cough, tells him she isn't afraid of anything: 'I'm on my way, anyhow. All they'd be doing would be hastening it.' A game of dare develops about phoning the police. Drunkenly, she takes the telephone and locks herself in the bedroom to dial. He batters on the door and then starts tugging on the telephone cable which he cannot see has become wound round her neck as she has flopped on the bed. 'This time, I was guilty. . . .' We leave Neal still on the road, unable to go to his girl with the murder rap hanging over him, knowing that 'some day a car will pick me up that I never thumbed'.

Even the relentlessly flip dialogue, derived at many removes from Raymond Chandler and now sounding uncomfortably dated, does little to detract from the pessimistic power of this blackest of Hollywood movies. The very simplicity imposed by its shoestring budget and sixty-eight-minute duration saves it from the rigged feeling of *You Only Live Once*. The film also demonstrates one common source of suspense in crime thrillers: put the hero in a situation where he has broken the law and his fate becomes very much more doubtful than it would be if he were simply a good guy. In *Detour*, it is panic that drives the hero to steal Haskell's possessions and assume his identity. More often, characters find themselves going against the law when they are driven to adopt unorthodox means to defend themselves or establish their innocence. Even going through the motions of a crime with the connivance of the law can be the source of considerable tension, as when Lee Remick has to take $100,000 from the bank where she works in *An Experiment in Terror*.

One of the standard gambits of the crime thriller is making the protagonist the man in the middle, at odds with both the law and the

Watched by Alfred Hitchcock's daughter Patricia, Robert Walker demonstrates strangulation to Norma Varden in *Strangers On a Train*.

heavies. A very unusual variant of this is to be seen in Delmer Daves's *Dark Passage* which is adapted from a novel by David Goodis, the source of a number of remarkable crime movies (others are Paul Wendkos's *The Burglar*, Jacques Tourneur's *Nightfall* and François Truffaut's *Shoot the Pianist*). *Dark Passage* is a vehicle for Humphrey Bogart and Lauren Bacall, and has Bogart having to act very much like a criminal in order to prove that he is innocent of the murder of his wife.

After serving five years of a life sentence in San Quentin, he manages to escape in a garbage-truck. He is sheltered by Lauren Bacall whose father died in jail, also convicted of wife murder. (Their meeting is produced by fate rather than design.) Bogart goes to a shady doctor who changes his appearance by plastic surgery – an echo perhaps of the operation performed on John Dillinger when he was on the run. Up to this point in the film, we have not seen Bogart's face, but now, under the sad clown mask of white bandages, the face is clearly his. He is sent off to recover with the one friend remaining from his past: 'Sleep flat on your back – get your friend to tie your hands to the bed so that you don't turn over.' But the friend has been murdered: 'They'll say I killed you, George. Just like they said I killed my wife.' Bogart's nightmarish progress leads to a confrontation with the wicked Agnes Moore-

35

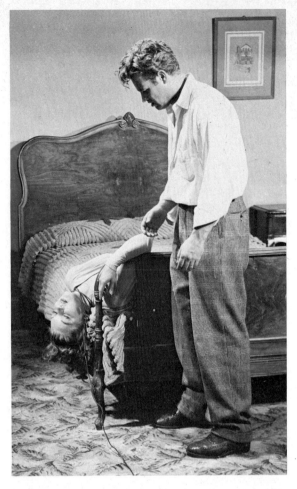

Tom Neal discovers that he has accidentally strangled Ann Savage in *Detour*.

The music changes to the swing theme that has been associated with them in the film. Cut to her standing in the doorway. They dance. Fade-out.

Apart from the innocent victims and sympathetic criminals, a third class of hero appears prominently in crime thrillers: the cop. In crime movies, as in life, the police are in a more exposed position than the ordinary citizen. Death in the line of duty has been meted out to cop heroes from Edward G. Robinson in *Bullets or Ballots* to Stacy Keach in *The New Centurions* and Robert Blake in *Electra Glide in Blue*. With the happy ending less mandatory for police than for other good people, they have often been the centre of particularly riveting crime thrillers.

One of the best is another low-budget movie, Richard Fleischer's *The Narrow Margin* (1952), in which two police officers have to take a gangster's widow by train to a Federal Grand Jury hearing. The unpleasantness of their task is quickly captured in a shot inside the cheap apartment from which they have to collect their charge. Behind the door lurks a sinister figure with a gun and a shoulder-holster. However, he turns out to be a cop. The first battle with the would-be assassins who have managed to find the hide-out results in the death of one of the two cops, who has been presented to us as the more sympathetic of the two. A relationship of mutual hostility quickly builds up between the widow and the surviving cop, whose dislike of the assignment is compounded by feelings of guilt. He tells the widow: 'My partner's dead. It's my fault. He's dead and you're alive.'

The uncertainties are heightened by brilliant casting. The woman, who is portrayed as loose and brassy, is played by Marie Windsor, an actress whose most striking appearances have been as female heavies – in *The Killing*, she was two-timing Elisha Cook Jr and planning to use the proceeds of the race-track robbery to take off with her lover. Here Miss Windsor's talent for withering nastiness gives force to the

head, who testified against Bogart at his trial, and to her death by falling through a window as she tries to escape from him. Now he knows Agnes Moorehead killed his wife but can never prove it. Although the situation seems unrelievedly bleak, the film has an economically presented happy ending. Bogart is sitting drinking a cocktail at night in a waterside restaurant to the sound of Latin American music (in his previous scene with Bacall, he has told her about a place he knows in Peru).

Lauren Bacall taking the bandages off Humphrey Bogart after his plastic surgery in *Dark Passage*.

woman's scorn for her bodyguard: she tells him that he is a fool not to make a deal with the gangsters on the train, a scheme that she favours. When one of the gangsters decides that a pleasant young woman with a small boy is the widow, after the detective has struck up a friendship with them on the train, Marie Windsor says unsympathetically, 'He thinks she's me and I think that's great.' The detective's only possible motivation in risking his life to protect this unpleasant piece of work is his sense of duty.

The detective, however, is played by Charles McGraw, whose forte at that time was thug heavies. Coupled with the detective's feelings about his job, McGraw's criminal typecasting underlines the possibility that he may give in to the threats and bribes offered by the gangsters. There are thus two suspenseful questions: the play of the various factors which conspire to erode McGraw's moral fibre is as important as the threat posed by the presence of assorted hoods on the train.

The plotting of the film uses the repertoire of suspense-building gambits to good effect. A suspicious fat guy turns out to be a railroad security man. A short suspense sequence is built up not around the life-and-death questions but with McGraw rummaging in a hood's jacket which has been hung up while its owner is in the washroom – McGraw is looking for a telegram which he has seen him pick up at one of the train's stops. The handling, too, is very apt: there is no music, and shots of the train rushing through the night are cut in suddenly as punctuation. The shape of the train also helps. Fast tracking shots of people rushing along narrow corridors help plant a feeling of panic,

and in general the confined space is used to keep the camera uncomfortably close to the characters. The length of the train adds a further element in drawing out the suspense: the time it takes to get from one part of the train to another.

Into this already tense situation the film throws a couple of developments for which we are absolutely unprepared. The Marie Windsor character is killed. Going through her possessions, McGraw finds her badge – she was a cop, working as a decoy. In the very next sequence, we learn that the nice young mother is actually the gangster's widow (but nice nevertheless). The Marie Windsor character has so closely fitted our and McGraw's preconception of what sort of woman would marry a gangster that he and we have been taken in completely. The ruse also suggests that McGraw's superiors have considered it a definite possibility that the hoods would succeed in getting their hands on his charge, whether by bribery or by violence.

The aim of the film is to have us so involved by the final do-or-die climax that we can no longer treat it with sophisticated detachment. We know that police are expendable – two out of three have perished. McGraw has no one to help him fight. The little boy is a further hazard: a would-be ally who cannot be trusted. There are more heavies, too, in cars driving along the road beside the railroad tracks. Some creepy images show black cars in the night, sliding into the picture, seen as reflections in the train windows. In spite of the odds stacked against them, the cop, the widow and child survive to arrive at their destination.

Since most of the films mentioned in this chapter were made, the cinema has changed,

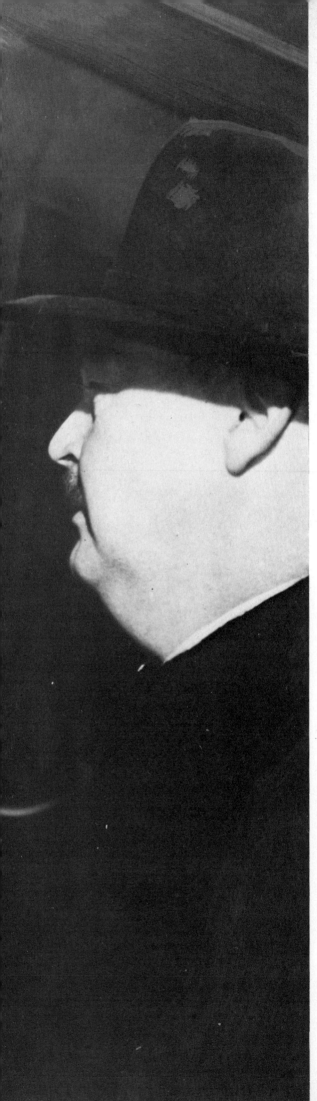

and many of the general observations I have made apply less and less to the current product. On the credit side, censorship has loosened to the extent that the Hays Code's elaborate pattern of general and specific prohibitions has been largely discarded. The big stars do not necessarily last throughout the movie – they may be guest stars who will be polished off very quickly. The habit of movie-going has disappeared entirely so that the iconographical background which the audience could be expected to provide in *The Narrow Margin* is no longer there (though it may to some extent be replaced through television).

There is one new source of suspense, though, which is simple apprehension about what one is going to see. Movies may not have got any better, but they have certainly got a whole lot beastlier. Now that abdominal injuries are likely to produce before your very eyes a glimpse of intestine (as in *Catch 22* and *The New Centurions*) and homicidal maniacs raining knife blows on their victims may hit them in the mouth (as in Brian Di Palma's *Sisters*), one does not have to be abnormally squeamish to feel on occasion a little edgy about what one may be about to see.

Charles McGraw and Marie Windsor in *The Narrow Margin*.

CRIME
& PUNISHMENT

Little Caesar was released three years before the end of Prohibition and when Americans had been patronising their neighbourhood boot-leggers for a decade. The Saint Valentine's Day Massacre was less than three years in the past, and Al Capone had not yet been convicted (in 1931, he got eight years for tax evasion). There was no need to spell out exactly what Rico Bandello and Diamond Pete Montana did for a living, as audiences would already be familiar with the operations of their real-life equivalents if only from the newspaper headlines. All we see of their professional activities are the clubs from which they operate and the battles between gangs. The American public could be expected to fill in enough of the other details for themselves, thus saving the film from an amount of exposition which would have slowed down the story-telling and probably produced trouble with the Hays Office.

The emphasis on the more striking aspects of crime at the expense of any analysis of its working put *Little Caesar* and many of its successors very much in the area of popular journalism. The similarity is increased by the hurried, urgent style with dialogue pared down to a functional minimum but still sharply evocative, the words rapped out at machine-gun speed.

The treatment was less that of the newspaper headlines than of the stories behind the headlines, the exposés and feature stories that translated the stark front-page reports into more personal terms. Though *Little Caesar* is not in its own right a particularly good movie, its success established the conventions of what was to all intents a new genre, one that used sound without getting paralysed by it. In

Edward G. Robinson as Rico Bandello with the other members of the gang in *Little Caesar*.

1931, Arthur Knight records, some fifty gangster pictures were produced as well as many more exposé pictures working along similar lines. In addition to *Little Caesar*'s two famous successors, William Wellman's *The Public Enemy* (1931) and Howard Hawks's *Scarface* (1932), 1931 and 1932 produced a widening range of crime subjects, as can be seen from a selection of titles: *The Gang Buster, Scandal Sheet, The Vice Squad, Graft, Hush Money, Star Witness, Undercover Man*, and *Docks of San Francisco*. *I Am a Fugitive from a Chain Gang* (1932), directed by Mervyn LeRoy who had made *Little Caesar*, set a pattern for extending the exposé movie away from the bootleggers and racketeers to other problems. Lynching was the subject of Michael Curtiz's *Black Fury* (1935), Fritz Lang's *Fury* (1936) and Mervyn LeRoy's *They Won't Forget* (1937). American Fascism in the shape of a renascent Ku Klux Klan was shown in Archie Mayo's *The Black Legion* (1936). The praiseworthy intentions of these pictures has led them probably to be overvalued by socially minded film historians, even those who have noted that the revelations in them are only halfway to being courageous.

The crime-movie cycle appears to have abated, though not to have died out, in 1933 and 1934. One could suggest various possible reasons. Possibly the cycle had simply worked itself out. Possibly the arrival of the Roosevelt administration and the New Deal spirit of optimism and co-operative effort rendered the spectacle of individual, anti-social profit rather less acceptable. Or perhaps censorship problems were making crime movies more difficult ventures for the producers. Arthur Knight notes that

Right: William Collier Jr as Tony, the gangster who turns yellow in *Little Caesar*.

'*Scarface* . . . was held up for several months until the producers inserted several placatory scenes showing an aroused citizenry demanding action against what the film's subtitle described as "the shame of a nation". Even with these additions, *Scarface* was severely censored in many communities, banned outright in others. As a result of such efforts the films became, if not more moral, at least more moralizing.' Tom Flinn has recorded that 'Before the censors got to *Scarface* and took out all the scenes in which Tony Camonte did anything that might possibly be deemed praiseworthy, it contained several scenes of him buying presents for his mother as well as scenes with his father (who doesn't even appear in the released version).'

A variant of the primitive crime movie appeared in the mid 'thirties – Knight dates its appearance as being in 1933, but its main products appear to have come a couple of years later than that. The central figures in films like William Keighley's *'G' Men* (1935) and *Bullets or Ballots* (1936) were not gangsters but agents of the law. Their relationship to the earlier gangster movies was stressed by stars who had made their names as gangsters moving over to represent the law: James Cagney plays the lead in *'G' Men*; Edward G. Robinson is a cop in *Bullets or Ballots*.

These movies relate interestingly to developments outside the sound-stages. The year 1934 had been a key one for crime in America. The FBI under J. Edgar Hoover (who had already been director of the FBI and its predecessor for ten years) had launched an attack on the most spectacular criminals around, the free-lance bank-robbers, and 1934 brought success

in the elimination of John Dillinger and Baby Face Nelson. But meanwhile, the big-time operators were setting about organising crime as it had never before been organised to form in 1934 the National Crime Syndicate, which had as its enforcement arm the group which was to become known as 'Murder Inc.' when its existence was revealed to the public in 1940. In the mid 'thirties, then, movies celebrating the law-enforcement agencies corresponded more with their public image than with the true state of affairs.

William Keighley was an extremely capable director – he made one of the best post-war crime movies in *Street with no Name* (1948) – and *Bullets or Ballots* is a very interesting movie, which can hardly be criticised for not being in possession of facts about the existence of nationally organised crime which did not become known outside the underworld until 1940. In other respects, it is remarkably accurate. It starts with the lead heavy Al Kruger (Barton MacLane) and his more brutal sidekick Bugs Fenner (Humphrey Bogart) going into a movie-house, asking 'What time does the crime picture start?' It turns out to be a short documentary exposé, apparently one of a series called Syndicate of Crime pictures. Being exposed is the vegetable racket which is run by Kruger and, we learn from the documentary, is collecting a quarter cent on every head of lettuce or $80,000 per week.

The film paints a very much blacker picture of the degree to which crime had infiltrated American life than the first-generation crime movies. It does so largely by offering very much more detail than, say, *Little Caesar* had

Eddie Woods and James Cagney in *Public Enemy*.

done. Kruger runs his operations with a business façade called Metropolitan Business Improvement Association Inc. The cop Blake (Edward G. Robinson) remarks that the rackets must be doing OK. 'Five thousand dollars a week,' Kruger tells him. 'Five hundred thousand dollars, more like,' says Blake. The scale of operations is repeatedly stressed: it is a $200,000,000 business. After Blake, having apparently been thrown out of the police force, goes to work for Kruger looking for the weak spots in his organisation, he is taken to the set-up's counting-house, which is hidden behind a garage and handles the money for 'all except a few of our regular corporations'. Kruger indicates the result of one cashier's tallying: '$310,396 – not bad for one week's take on pinball machines.' 'I wouldn't cry about it,' says Blake.

The picture of crime has come a long way from the hoods who run speakeasies and mainly shoot each other. The regular corporations are only one side of the permeation of society. Behind the Kruger mob are not more hoodlums but ostensibly respectable citizens – three cigar-smoking, conservatively dressed pillars of society who run the Oceanic Bank and Trust. The idea of the bankers financing the criminals is one which might well have keyed in well with hostility towards the heavyweights of finance in the New Deal period. With hindsight one can note that the true state of affairs was even gloomier than *Bullets or Ballots* painted it: it was less a case of the bankers running the hoods than vice versa – the Depression had provided organised crime with its great entrée into legitimate business, as the hoods were the only people with plenty of liquid cash.

Elsewhere, though, the film is very much more on the mark about contemporary corruption than one can imagine any, say, British or French film being then or now. It emerges that it had cost $2,000,000 to buy Bugs Fenner out of a scrape with the Grand Jury over his milk racket, and the next Grand Jury is likely to cost an extra million. The following scene brings confirmation from the man brought in to clean up the police department that even previous Grand Juries were probably reached by corruption.

The gravity of the problem is confirmed by the degree of sacrifice needed to expose it. Blake has to go through the process of getting thrown out of the police force, and thereby

Opposite: Osgood Perkins (father of Anthony Perkins), Paul Muni and Karen Morley in *Scarface*.

Paul Muni and Karen Morley in *Black Fury*.

47

Lynch mob in *Fury*.

Paul Muni in *I Am a Fugitive from a Chain Gang*.

Opposite page, top:
Humphrey Bogart in *Black Legion. Below and right:*
Edward G. Robinson and Barton MacLane in *Bullets or Ballots*.

finding a place with Kruger whom he has known since they were kids. (Robinson's criminal typecasting is used here to make us accept that he has really joined the mob.) To trap the Kruger gang, he has to suggest that they move in on a numbers game which his friend Joan Blondell has going in Harlem. Blake's position as an undercover man is threatened by the gang's wire-tapping ability. In setting up a situation which will nail the bankers as well as the gang, he is fatally wounded, but manages to complete his part and shoot Fenner before he dies.

By the late 'thirties, the facts of Prohibition and the Depression were no longer current, and Raoul Walsh's *The Roaring Twenties* (1939) takes care to provide reminders of the historical facts of the period. It also gives a direct, largely sociological explanation of how a nice guy like James Cagney came back from the war and ended up as a bootlegger.

In the 'thirties, films dealing with lynch-law or the re-emergence of the Klan tended to present these things not primarily in terms of crimes against individuals or particular sections of the community but as attacks on

America itself, on the ideals embodied in the American Constitution. This view is made particularly clear in the homily delivered by the judge to the members of the Black Legion, a speech which inevitably quotes Abraham Lincoln. Organised crime is presented as an attack on American society in *Bullets or Ballots*, implicitly in the film but explicitly in the title. One threat to American society, though, was largely avoided by Hollywood's exposés: the lack of interest it displayed in the Nazi menace was probably a business consideration – anti-Nazi films could bring trouble and therefore loss of profits. Indeed, both the *March of Time* episode *Inside Nazi Germany* (1938) and Charles Chaplin's *The Great Dictator* (1940) were banned by the local censorship board in Chicago. Anatole Litvak's *Confessions of a Nazi Spy* (1939) seems to have been the only exposé movie before Pearl Harbor to portray Nazism as a direct threat to America.

With America's entry into the Second World War, however, the crime movie came quickly to embrace espionage and sabotage by enemy agents. A good proportion of the 375 Hollywood movies with an overtly patriotic purpose which 'Hollywood Quarterly' estimated were made in the years 1942–44 were crime movies or thrillers. An early arrival was Alfred Hitchcock's *Saboteur* (1942) in which Robert Cummings is wrongly suspected of arson in a munitions factory, although the fire has killed his best friend. Trying to prove his innocence while on the run, he unearths a German sabotage

organisation which is managed from the New York mansions of a wealthy socialite.

The ultimate crime now was working for the enemy, and even the criminals like 'Gloves' Donahue (Humphrey Bogart) in *All through the Night* (1942) used their skills to fight Nazi infiltration. Later, in the Cold War, Samuel Fuller's *Pick Up on South Street* (1953) had its pickpocket hero (Richard Widmark) moving from disinterest to confrontation with the Red spy ring led by Richard Kiley. His conversion is largely the work of Jean Peters, who has been an unwitting tool of the spies. She will go along with her part while she thinks Kiley is in industrial espionage but is repelled by the idea of collaborating with Red agents – she has shown Widmark pictures of her brother Nicky who is 'a war hero in Korea'. The idea of the crime beyond all other crimes is an effective propaganda device but it also has non-political antecedents in the underworld's hunt for the sadistic child-killer in Fritz Lang's German picture *M* (1931).

The crime beyond crime idea appears in a rather different guise in Frank Tuttle's film version of Graham Greene's *This Gun for Hire* (1942). In this Alan Ladd, in the part which established him as a star, plays a professional assassin whom we see at the start of the film carrying out a contract. The real heavies, however, are his customers, whose front man is the smooth, portly Laird Cregar, an effete character who abhors violence and has a penchant for

Opposite page: Robert Cummings and Priscilla Lane in *Saboteur* (*top*), Peter Lorre in Fritz Lang's *M*.

Left: Broderick Crawford and John Ireland in Robert Rossen's *All the King's Men* (1950).

Ginger Rogers and the Ku Klux Klan in *Storm Warning*.

51

Wounded racialist criminal and black doctor: Richard Widmark, Linda Darnell and Sidney Poitier in Joseph L. Mankiewicz's *No Way Out* (1950).

chocolate peppermints – we see him settling down in the sleeping-car of a train with a box of candy and a book called 'Paris Nights'. Cregar is employed by a chemical corporation presided over from an elaborately mechanised wheelchair by the aged, decrepit Tully Marshall. Ladd's contract has not merely involved murder but also the retrieval of a document describing in pages of figures and formulae the preparation of bromine – the chemical works is experimenting with poison gas, and Marshall and his associates are Nazi sympathisers. Ladd's motives for going against them are far from pure patriotism (as are Widmark's in *Pick Up on South Street*). Although he has feelings for

Beatrice Pearson and Thomas Gomez in *Force of Evil* (1948), the only film directed by Abraham Polonsky before he became a black-list victim – his next direction credit came in 1969.

the heroine, Veronica Lake, he remains an unregenerate killer: in escaping from the police to get to the heavies, he shoots a cop. Yet he is the emotional centre of the film: Robert Preston, Veronica Lake's detective fiancé, is a routine nice guy of little interest. Focusing our identification on a killer gives us an emotional scale against which to set the vileness of the heavies.

After the Germans and Japanese had capitulated there was no longer a universally recognised enemy against whom the propaganda in Hollywood movies could be directed. Rather than disappearing, the political content diverged in post-war product, either exposing evils in the fabric of American society or seeing threats to the nation from outside. The first group took up an approach which had been in abeyance since John Ford's *The Grapes of Wrath* (1940), which on the whole they follow in moving away from the exposé format. However, Elia Kazan's *Boomerang* (1947) is built round a crime-movie situation – a man wrongly accused of murder – although the film is less concerned with him than with the State's Attorney and the local political power structure. These films have tended to become identified with the liberals who were soon to be marked down as Communists by the House Committee on Un-American Activities (HUAC). The

and there were many of them – could find powerful reinforcement for their view in the events of the day. While there were certainly commie-baiting exploitation movies made in a spirit of total cynicism, there is no reason to believe that most of the anti-Communist movies of the Cold War period were any less sincerely meant than the socially critical movies. However, they were also in general cheaper, less intelligently made and a whole lot more lurid.

In their book 'Politics and Film', the Swedish film historians Leif Furhammar and Folke Isaksson mention a few of these now forgotten movies made in the straightforward crime exposé mould which was becoming increasingly the prerogative of the B-feature. They describe William Cameron Menzies's *Whip Hand* (1951) as 'a lugubrious story . . . showing the communists running a prison camp in a small provincial American community with the object of testing biological weapons on the inmates. In *I Was A Communist for the FBI* (1951), an FBI agent manages to infiltrate the Communist Party where he meets, among others, Gerhardt Eisler, head of the East German security service, who is provoking riots; one of the members tells how they caught up with Trotsky who thought he'd got away, and that Jan Masaryk was thrown out of a window – people thought it was suicide.' The FBI itself helped in the making of Alfred Werker's *Walk East of Beacon* (1952), an anti-Communist movie based on a book by J. Edgar Hoover – the attention that he paid to such matters is renowned: as late as 1959, the FBI's New York Office had only four agents assigned to deal with organised crime (in which Hoover did not believe) as against over 400 devoted to fighting Communism on the home

generalisation is not entirely true: the post-war successor to *The Black Legion* was Stuart Heisler's *Storm Warning* (1951) which concerned the Ku Klux Klan itself and starred Ginger Rogers (whose mother was one of the star friendly performers before HUAC), Ronald Reagan, Doris Day and Steve Cochran.

The successors to the wartime crime movies were, however, clearly right wing in inspiration. They cannot be blamed directly on HUAC, which had been operating in the 'thirties, but relate to the same historical developments that encouraged HUAC's rise to power after the war. The United States had emerged from a war which had produced more than three times as many American casualties as the First World War to find itself in a state of increasing confrontation with Russia. Eighteen months after VJ Day, the Truman Doctrine set out plans for giving economic and military aid to countries threatened by Communism and 1948–49 brought the Russian blockade of West Berlin and the airlifts. In 1950, the Korean War began and, on the domestic front, Alger Hiss was convicted of perjury in denying he had been a Communist. The following year, the Rosenbergs were convicted as atom spies (they were executed in 1953). People who saw Communism as the ultimate threat to civilisation –

Led by Humphrey Bogart and Lauren Bacall, Hollywood personalities including Danny Kaye and Richard Conte go to Washington to protest against the HUAC hearings on the film industry.

One black-list victim, John Garfield, in a film (his last) directed by another, John Berry: *He Ran All the Way* (1951), with Gladys George.

53

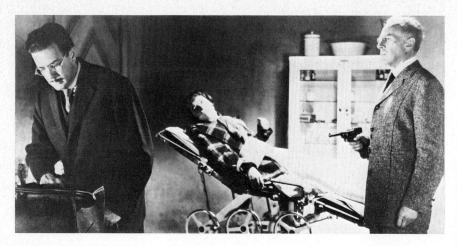

Raymond Burr in *Whip Hand*.

front. According to Furhammar and Isaksson, the fear 'of communist infiltrators inside the United States . . . seems to have reached the height of its naivety on film in *The Red Menace* (1949), which provided intimately detailed information about communist blackmailing methods, psychopathy, godlessness and promiscuity.'

Apart from *Pick Up on South Street* which has Richard Widmark as its star and happens to be a good movie, the only one of the Cold War crime pictures to have survived even on television is Edward Ludwig's *Big Jim McLain* (1952) produced by and starring the biggest commie-hater of them all, John Wayne. This is an extremely undistinguished B-feature set in Hawaii with Wayne unerringly tracking down and pulverising the Reds who have been planning all manner of nasty tricks like poisoning the water in the harbours.

The post-war social conscience cycle and the Cold War cycle both encompassed only a modest number of films and lasted only a few years. A much more influential development came out of wartime film-making; this was less a matter of theme than of ambience, of a search for authenticity through the use of location shooting. These days, with only television work coming between most surviving film studios and redevelopment as real estate, filming in actual locations is such a commonplace that it is difficult to realise how striking it must have seemed in the mid 'forties. The classic 'thirties crime movie had been very much the creature of

James Stewart as a reporter proving the innocence of a man wrongly imprisoned for murder in *Call Northside 777*.

the sound-stages – little happened that actually demanded a setting beyond the skills of the art department, and most of the exteriors took place in the curiously anonymous town sets that stood permanently on the backlots.

The movie which gained its reputation by pioneering the 'documentary approach' was *The House on 92nd Street* which was produced by Louis de Rochemont, who had devised the *March of Time* documentary series, and directed by Henry Hathaway who had earlier made the first location-shot film in Technicolor, *The Trail of the Lonesome Pine* (1936). The story, about a Nazi spy ring run by Signe Hasso under the cover of a fashion house, was taken from the files of the FBI which co-operated in the filming – the use of the story's actual backgrounds was only one side of its emphasis on authenticity. One can imagine that the Bureau's motive in supporting such a film was to counterbalance the highly coloured picture of Nazi spies given by films like *Saboteur* or *This Gun for Hire* with an image which might persuade audiences that espionage was a genuine threat (although by the time that the film emerged, the war was over).

However the treatment of *The House on 92nd Street* may have been motivated, some degree of documentary styling quickly became *de rigueur* for crime movies. Henry Hathaway made a straight crime picture, *Call Northside 777* (1948) in this way, and Louis de Rochemont went on to produce Elia Kazan's *Boomerang*, which was filmed entirely on location in Stamford, Con-

looks as if they wanted to offer a documentary impression of city life, an expansion of the city sequences in the much-admired documentary by Willard Van Dyke and Ralph Steiner, *The City* (1939), but were stuck with having to make what Arthur Knight called an ordinary cops-and-robbers picture. It is the sort of movie in which someone has only to dial a number for us to be treated to a documentary montage of the operations of the Bell Telephone Company. Even the staging of the final chase on the Brooklyn Bridge is calculated less to fit the demands of the story than to provide a climactic eyeful of townscape. The undigested lumps of documentary keep getting in the way of the narrative, which is thus supposed to appear as a fragment exemplifying the teeming life of the city. The film ends with a garbage-man sweeping up a paper with a headline about the outcome of the case. 'There are eight million stories in the naked city – this has been one of them.'

The presence of a narrator is another piece of documentary styling. The friendly, rather patronising voice does rather more than narrate – he also addresses rhetorical questions to the characters ('How are your feet holding out, Halloran?'). His main function, though, particularly at the beginning of the film, is to spell out the mechanics of the investigation. And here *Naked City* is very much in tune with one of the concerns of post-war crime movies, with the logistics of lawbreaking and law enforcement, with the organisation and mechanics of crime.

necticut. With the real locations came a more direct photographic treatment, the beginning of a move away from the airbrushed exquisiteness of cinematography as it had developed in the studios. Kazan, who made *Boomerang* after doing a movie for MGM, worked with Norbert Brodine, the director of photography on *The House on 92nd Street.* 'On *Sea of Grass*', Kazan said in an interview with Stuart Byron and Martin Rubin, 'I was initiated into all that careful back-lighting and halo-lighting and line-lighting and so on. But the cameraman on *Boomerang* was an old guy who just put the camera down and turned the box on. And it looked much better to me than the other!'

The attractions of the documentary treatment seem to have hooked most of the leading directors of crime movies in the late 'forties. Although the approach was generally beneficial in exposing Hollywood film-makers to the polluted atmosphere of the East Coast cities and taking their stories out of the necessarily simplified environment that could be constructed in the studios, it was not without its risks. Its most famous product, Jules Dassin's *The Naked City* (1948), was also the film in which it got furthest out of hand. The copyright summary nicely expresses the problem: 'A picture about New York City and its people, photographed on actual settings. The work of the New York Homicide Department in locating a murderer furnishes material for the plot.' The movie gives the impression that the summary expresses the makers' order of priorities: it

Frank Lovejoy as the FBI agent with Eddie Norris in *I Was a Communist for the FBI.*

In the 'thirties crime movies, the emphasis seemed to be on the existential aspect of the action. Things happen: cops follow up leads and hoods do jobs, but the apparatus that has produced the leads and the planning that goes into the jobs are largely taken for granted – the narrative line is restricted to characters and action. In a film like *'G' Men*, a typical development will take us straight from a scene in which one of a group of heavies says how much he likes the climate in Kansas City and that he's thinking of opening up a bank to a shot of a bank with sounds of shooting.

It is tempting to attribute the concern with logistics to the background of wartime experience; since its spectacular emergence in Robert Siodmak's *The Killers* (1946), the feeling for logistics has persisted in crime movies right into the 'seventies. Apart from the pretty powerful refresher courses in the logistics of war that history has provided in the intervening years, there has also been occasional cross-

pollination between war and crime movies (even a feeble British effort, Basil Dearden's *The League of Gentlemen* (1960) had a team of wartime comrades forming up again to execute a robbery). Robert Aldrich's *The Dirty Dozen* (1967) put Lee Marvin in command of a squad of assorted delinquents using their criminal skills under military training and discipline to complete a near-suicidal mission behind enemy lines. More recently, Ossie Davis's *Gordon's War* (1973) pits a quartet of Vietnam veterans with their experience and a remarkable amount of weaponry against the drug rackets in Harlem.

The iconographical development of film genres has tended towards a pattern of establishment followed by assumption: things which have to be described in detail early in a cycle of films can increasingly be taken for granted later on – or could be in the days of habitual movie-going. So the persistence of the logistics thing suggests that it is pretty important. In

little interest and partly because it again has to do with logistics. The caper movie developed in the second half of the 'fifties. Given the degree of identification with the characters that can be generated in many big robbery sequences, it is hardly a big leap to movies that combine this appeal with sympathetic and even glamorous characters – in caper movies it is the heroes and heroines that pull the big jobs. A representative sample of this group might include Lewis Milestone's *Ocean's 11* (1960), Jules Dassin's *Topkapi* (1964), William Wyler's *How to Steal a Million* (1966) and Norman Jewison's *The Thomas Crown Affair* (1968). These were much glossier productions than the average crime movie, often featuring exotic locales, from Las Vegas to Istanbul. The trouble with the caper movie was that having got us worked up on behalf of these nice people who were doing some fun thing like robbing a museum or a bank, the well-laid plans had to come to grief some time before the end title, leaving everyone thoroughly disappointed.

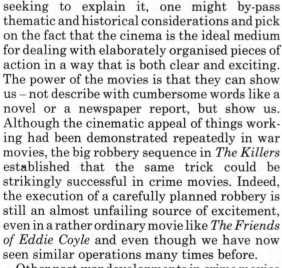

seeking to explain it, one might by-pass thematic and historical considerations and pick on the fact that the cinema is the ideal medium for dealing with elaborately organised pieces of action in a way that is both clear and exciting. The power of the movies is that they can show us – not describe with cumbersome words like a novel or a newspaper report, but show us. Although the cinematic appeal of things working had been demonstrated repeatedly in war movies, the big robbery sequence in *The Killers* established that the same trick could be strikingly successful in crime movies. Indeed, the execution of a carefully planned robbery is still an almost unfailing source of excitement, even in a rather ordinary movie like *The Friends of Eddie Coyle* and even though we have now seen similar operations many times before.

Other post-war developments in crime movies will be dealt with in subsequent chapters. One, however, is worth disposing of here, partly because the movies produced within it are of

The most ingenious solution to this problem was devised by Sidney Boehm for Henry Hathaway's *Seven Thieves* (1960), which Boehm produced as well as wrote. Compared to the films just mentioned, it was a cut-priced effort filmed in black and white against a largely back-projected French Riviera. It manages to avoid the disappointment problem by having Rod Steiger and Joan Collins, prompted by the death from natural causes of Steiger's father Edward G. Robinson, decide to put the casino's money back, so that there can be a further measure of suspense ending in success and happily ever after. The usual treatment has been to allow the characters to complete their caper and then to provide an ingenious trick ending to relieve them of the loot. We are unlikely to feel very strongly about the characters as the far-fetched action will probably have been presented in comedy-thriller form, a convention which in most hands turns out with the laughs undermining the involvement necessary to make the thrills work. In such a half-baked context, mere lack of success seems enough punishment for the caperers – an idea which would never have got by the stern moralists of the old Hays Office. Even such a weedy genre as the caper movie was helping to whittle away at censorship demands by subverting the principle that lawbreaking automatically meant retribution in the movies. By 1972, there was nothing left of this principle: it was even possible to rob banks, killing a number of people along the way, and end up getting away with the money. It is remarkable that Steve McQueen's success in this line in *The Getaway* (1972) and Walter Matthau's in *Charley Varrick* (1973) seem to have elicited protest from nobody at all.

Opposite: Michael Dante and Eli Wallach in *Seven Thieves*.

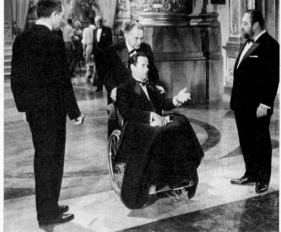

Edward G. Robinson and Eli Wallach in *Seven Thieves*.

VIOLENCE

VIOLENCE

At the beginning of Ossie Davis's *Gordon's War* (1973), Vietnam veteran Paul Winfield tracks down the pusher whose wares have been the cause of his wife's death. There ensues a beating which ends with our hero propping up the heels of the supine Big Pink on a box, then stamping on his legs. For a 1973 movie, this intentional leg breaking is by no means an exceptional piece of violence even in showing how it is done. Before Don Siegel's *Dirty Harry* (1971), it would have been remarkable; before Arthur Penn's *Bonnie and Clyde* (1967), quite unthinkable. In earlier films, pieces of extreme and gratuitous violence were depicted with some tact, keeping the points of impact largely offscreen, and such things could carry considerable weight because they were seen as quite exceptional. Even in an unusually violent 'fifties western, Anthony Mann's *The Man from Laramie* (1955), it is a pivotally horrifying moment when Alex Nicol shoots a hole at close range in James Stewart's hand to compensate for a hand injury caused him by Stewart (who was defending himself against Nicol and his henchmen). The crippling of Big Pink, however, does not have this force – it is just another incident, not meant in any way to turn us against Winfield. The film shows it as the sort of thing one might expect any nice able-bodied guy to do in the circumstances.

The 1973 level of violence in films like *Gordon's War*, Phil Karlson's *Walking Tall* and John Milius's *Dillinger* comes after (but probably not at the end of) a steady escalation of violence since the days of *Little Caesar*. The restaurant stick-up in that film is hardly shown at all: the action is treated in a series of quick dissolves. As far as possible, 'thirties films

Previous page: Public Enemy.
Right: The Valachi Papers.

62

David Downing and Paul Winfield in *Gordon's War*.

Clint Eastwood catches up with Andy Robinson in *Dirty Harry*.

avoided showing people being hit by bullets, even if this involved recourse to cinematic devices that, censorship considerations apart, looked gratuitously arty. In *'G' Men*, James Cagney's law school buddy, Regis Toomey, now a Federal agent, is shot down by Barton MacLane who has been watching from an upstairs window as Toomey apprehends one of his criminal colleagues. We see a shot of MacLane at the window aiming his rifle, then a shot of a wall with the shadows of two men, one walking closely behind the other. The back one slumps and falls.

Even without such obviously oblique methods of presentation, shootings were conveniently handled to put the actual impact offscreen and to minimise its physical effect. The standard (and Code-satisfying) depiction of a shooting shows us the shooter while he is firing and cuts to the target, if at all, only after he has been hit to let us see him clutch the wound and totter off or keel over. Conspicuously absent from this con-ventionalised shooting, particularly in 'thirties movies, is blood (not to mention brains, bone fragments and any of the other goodies that might be spread around by a shot fired at close range). Apart from honest fisticuffs, supple-mented perhaps with the use of any items of furniture that came to hand, shooting was more or less unrivalled in the field of 'thirties violence – the cinema does not seem to have recognised such contemporary criminal practices as, say, garrotting. (One partial exception to the blood-lessness was Archie Mayo's *Doorway to Hell*, which appeared just under three months before gangster movies hit the big time with *Little Caesar*.)

Joe Don Baker as Buford Pusser in *Walking Tall* (*above and left*).

Edward G. Robinson as Rico behind the advertisement hoarding at the end of *Little Caesar*.

Violence in 'thirties movies, then, was expressed not so much through the visible evidence of its effects as through displays of firepower. The central images are of black sedans and blasting away with assorted artillery, whether by hoods or by cops. Very often, the results of the gunfire are not shown at all but are reported in newspaper headlines that are hurled at us – a film like *'G' Men* is peppered with front

65

pages and ticker tape. This trick avoided censor problems and also tied the cinematic fiction firmly to its real context, which for most of the audience would come to them in newspaper and radio reports. As the stories were frequently fictionalisations of current or at least recent events in the world of crime, the effects of violence, which were lavishly displayed in the press, could to some extent be taken for granted in the movies.

Because of the reliance on audience exposure to the news media, the impact of these films was very much of their time and is largely lost today. Even more difficult to assess now is the importance to the early 'thirties gangster movies of the newness of sound film as a medium. In what was one of the first purpose-built talkie genres, the immediacy and the recognisable contemporary ambience may have in themselves formed such a potent combination that the

necessary effect on the audience could be achieved by actually showing very little. The predominant feeling of early 'thirties gangster movies seen in the mid 'seventies is not of violence, in spite of the volume of gunfire, but of speed – rapid dialogue, short scenes, abbreviated action sequences. They seem almost like movies in note form, which is never fully developed.

From this start, crime films could only evolve towards greater elaboration, towards showing more. Increasing violence was one aspect of this change. The way in which crime movies became more visibly violent is very difficult to pin down. The process, limited until the early 'thirties by the dictates of the Production Code, was shared between crime movies and other forms, war films and westerns. It is not useful to evaluate it in terms of censorship detail; each specific breach of restrictions one may note

Alan Ladd and Veronica Lake in *This Gun for Hire*.

apparently getting through for the first time will very possibly have been antedated in some more obscure effort or (particularly in the case of violence in British prints of American films) have been allowed in its native country for some time while still being excised elsewhere. A further complication when looking at censorship is in the hotter versions that are sometimes cooked up for export to markets where something sexier or beastlier is likely to get past the censor. In any case, the specific firsts are not very significant in themselves. Martin Ritt's *The Brotherhood* (1968) seems to have offered Hollywood's first rendering of a Mafia roping – we see quite enough (including the finished package) to show us that Kirk Douglas has tied a slip knot round Luther Adler's neck and tied the other end of the rope tautly to Adler's ankles which are pulled up behind him. The victim's struggles serve only to tighten the

Above: Robert Mitchum in *Out of the Past. Left:* Brian Donlevy and Alan Ladd in *The Glass Key.*

Far left: Orson Welles in *The Lady From Shanghai. Left:* Robert Stack as an undercover agent in Robert Ryan's militarily organised gang of robbers who work in Tokyo in Samuel Fuller's *House of Bamboo* (1955), with Shirley Yamaguchi.

Edmond O'Brien and James Cagney in *White Heat*.

noose so that he soon strangles himself. But even such a striking first – if indeed it was a first – is not of great importance except in the context of the particular movie.

The growth of film violence has to be viewed in a more general and less tangible way: we are dealing here with an evolutionary process affecting crime movies *en masse* over some decades of continuous production. The effects of this violence are less the concern of the film critic than of the social psychologist. It is worth pointing out, though, that film (and television) violence is not born in a vacuum. It is an echo, often a very distant echo, of violence in the world at large, and survives only because it is accepted by mass audiences. This acceptance in turn seems to be related to exposure to

Jane Greer and Robert Mitchum in *The Big Steal*.

Opposite: Robert Mitchum, Jane Greer and Kirk Douglas in *Out of the Past*.

Dana Andrews as the tough cop in *Where the Sidewalk Ends*, with Gary Merrill and Neville Brand (*above*), and Gene Tierney (*opposite*).

violence, whether directly through the Second World War, Korea or Vietnam, or indirectly through the media.

Certainly, the crime movie emerged from the Second World War considerably more violent than before. The new concern with the logistics of crime resulted in greater involvement in its violence. Although the depiction of injury and death is not necessarily much more realistic than it had been in the 'thirties, much more attention is paid to the results of violence: coverage of such things is no longer restricted largely to the climactic death. Instead of being informed of death as a fact, we witness dying (albeit depicted with some decorousness) as an action. But the change was very much more fundamental than the details of what was shown. There was a new desperateness of feeling: the violence was emotional as well as physical to a far greater extent than in 'thirties movies (though it is approached in *Bullets or Ballots*).

One of the favourite themes of propagandist war films is patriotic self-sacrifice. In a film like Tay Garnett's *Bataan* (1943), the heroes' final satisfaction is not survival, as Lawrence Alloway has pointed out in his monograph

Marie Windsor and Arthur Franz as *The Sniper*.

'Violent America: The Movies 1946–64', but a costly defeat, taking large numbers of Japanese soldiers with them. The latter days of the Second World War brought a rather more disillusioned war film which paid as much attention to the cost as to the patriotic glory (an attitude which was admissible only when American forces had established a dominant position). Alloway continues: 'in a film of 1945 the title itself, *They Were Expendable*, declares a notion of human life as not an absolute value. The film deals with a delaying action in the Pacific, the heroes of which are nonessential. . . . The mortality of men in war is matched by the increased vulnerability of heroes and also by their contaminated origins. A film of 1942, *This Gun for Hire*, is apposite here: Alan Ladd plays the central character, a hired killer, in the role that made him a star. This is an early example of popular culture's adoption of the anti-hero. In *The Glass Key*, of the same year, Ladd moved from anti-hero to hero, though of an amoral sort. The central point of the latter film is his beating up (including a swollen face and shuffling walk), an episode treated at more length than was customary at the time. In *The Fallen Sparrow*, 1943, John Garfield played an early neurotic hero (sweaty face, trembling hands), hounded by memories of his torture in prison after the Spanish Civil War. The hero has a past which is the source of his vulnerability. In 1946 Burt Lancaster's role in *The Killers* expanded the theme of the vulnerable hero: his part is that of one of the most elaborate losers in the whole dark genre. Losing on this scale has a paranoid grandeur in its conspiratorial and threatening completeness.

'This is the period of the fall guy (that is, the man to be framed), a term first connected with two films from Dashiell Hammett novels. In *The Maltese Falcon* (1941), the character proposed for framing is a minor gunman, but in *The Glass Key*, framing is in the foreground as a technique of the hero's. The psychological consequence of framing is to convert society into an unreliable and malicious place in which guilt can be manipulated and assigned to sacrificial victims. It is the civilian equivalent of expendability. . . . The late 'forties has the most spectacular of these, including *Dark Corner*, 1946, *Out of the Past*, 1947, *Dark Passage*, 1947, *The Lady from Shanghai*, 1948, and *D.O.A.*, 1949. The fall guy is in theory the innocent bystander, but there is a new emphasis on the ambiguity of the line between innocence and guilt and on the danger of arbitrary classification. Associated with this is the shakiness of a society that tolerates these masquerades. . . . Late in the 'forties Richard Widmark's career developed in a comparable way to Ladd's . . . common to both actors are their emergence from villain to hero roles and their extension of tensions and violence into the formerly more placid postures of the hero figure. The cumulative effect of such actors and films was to expose audiences to the spectacle of violence and death in a context of psychic depth, institutional doubt, and existential

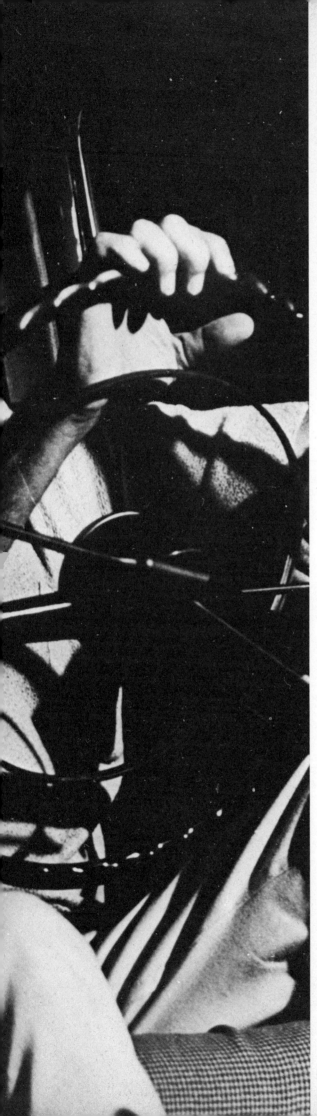

solitude.'

Alongside the vulnerable hero and the fall guy in the gallery of post-war crime-movie characters one might place the undercover agent, the counterfeit criminal whose job is to befriend others, to gain their confidence for the sole purpose of bringing them to justice (i.e. betraying them). Again there is an antecedent to be found in the 'thirties, almost inevitably in *Bullets or Ballots*, in which Edward G. Robinson's expulsion from the police force is faked so that he can get in with racketeer Barton MacLane. A more immediate predecessor, though, is the wartime spy movie, *The House on 92nd Street* (1945), in which FBI agent William Eythe penetrates a German spy ring in New York. In the realms of civilian crime, the undercover men like Mark Stevens in *The Street with no Name* (1948), Glenn Ford in *Undercover Man* (1949) and Edmond O'Brien in *White Heat* (1949) entered into closer relationships with their targets, producing a degree of moral ambiguity which was hardly apparent in *The House on 92nd Street*.

The post-war years, up to the mid 'fifties were the heyday of what the French call the *film noir*, of a pessimism composed of uncertainty, betrayal and desperation. The most extreme example is *Detour*, though some of the fall-guy movies like Jacques Tourneur's *Out of the Past* (in Britain called *Build My Gallows High*, 1947) and Robert Siodmak's *Criss Cross* (1949) in which the fall guy does not manage to extract himself are close behind. The pessimism of *films noirs* often transcended their happy endings, as in Otto Preminger's *Where the Sidewalk Ends* (1950), in which the hero, a tough cop (Dana Andrews) accidentally kills a suspect and eventually atones by seeking his own death in a confrontation that will also give the police department the evidence to nail a particularly noxious hoodlum.

Robert Mitchum with Gregory Peck (*above*) and Barrie Chase (*opposite*) in *Cape Fear*.

Sniper's view in Peter Bogdanovich's *Targets*.

Barbara Anderson, Don Galloway and Raymond Burr in *A Man Called Ironside*.

In the dark and violent world of the post-war crime movie, the Bugsy Siegel dictum that we (the hoods) only kill each other ceased to apply. The violence extended to such innocent parties as the wives of determined cops like Darren McGavin in Paul Wendkos's *The Case Against Brooklyn* (1958) and Glenn Ford in Fritz Lang's *The Big Heat* (1953), blown up by bombs respectively in a telephone and a car. In Budd Boetticher's *The Killer Is Loose* (1956), Wendell Corey sets out to even the score by killing not Joseph Cotten who was responsible for his imprisonment but Cotten's wife (Rhonda Fleming) – Corey's wife was accidentally killed by Cotten. (The same gambit appears in J. Lee Thompson's *Cape Fear* (1961), a more elaborate but less successful treatment with Robert Mitchum aiming to revenge himself on Gregory Peck.) In a way, the ultimate expression of the violence and uncertainty of the ambience in

Don Siegel (*left*) during the shooting of a sequence in *Coogan's Bluff* with Clint Eastwood.

these films lies in this idea of the killer on the prowl, somewhere in the city (but where?) and liable to strike at any time (but when?). The atmosphere of these films is sufficiently oppressive to convey a feeling of violence as being endemic in the cities. This takes an even more alarming form when the violence is apparently arbitrary as it is at the beginning of *An Experiment in Terror* when we have no idea why Lee Remick has been set upon.

The key image of urban violence is perhaps that of the sniper – the man who either quite randomly or according to some rationale of his own kills total strangers. In Edward Dmytryk's *The Sniper* (1952), Arthur Franz's operations against women are explained in the psychological terms that movies were using around that time (the film also had one incident sufficiently striking to remain among my few memories of the film from a single viewing almost twenty years ago – the protagonist pressing his hands on a lighted gas-stove in the hope that he can alert doctors to his plight). In the mid 'sixties, there was a multiple killing by a sniper shooting from the tower of the university campus at Houston, Texas, who is echoed – but not re-created – in the young sniper of Peter Bogdanovich's *Targets* (1968). Unlike Dmytryk's sniper, Bogdanovich's is not explained – the action is as arbitrary as its choice of victims. The same is true of the sniper in Don Siegel's *Dirty Harry* (1971); although his object is to extort $100,000 from the city of San Francisco, he clearly derives some satisfaction from his efforts – his demand note after the first killing says that he will enjoy killing a person a day.

In the mid 'fifties, a whole string of film titles built up a red-in-tooth-and-claw picture of the big cities – various aspects of urban life were presented in this context in *The Human Jungle* (1954), *Blackboard Jungle* (1955), *The Square Jungle* (1956) and *The Steel Jungle* (1956). The idea of the city as a jungle was explicit in these titles and to some extent implied in films like *The Killer Is Loose* and Samuel Fuller's *The Crimson Kimono* (1959) which starts with the killing of a burlesque dancer who runs out of the theatre to be shot down in her working clothes on the street by a person unknown. To the two cops and the girl who can identify the probable killer, the city is a hostile environment in which the cops' flat is an enclave of defensible space (later, in the television series *Ironside*, Raymond Burr's apartment/office is frequently seen in the same light).

The feeling of the city as a jungle has been very much to the fore in 'seventies crime movies – in black pictures, but above all in police films. This was foreshadowed in some late 'sixties movies such as Don Siegel's *Coogan's Bluff* (1968), in which Clint Eastwood is a sheriff who does very nicely on his native western terrain but has a lot more trouble when a case takes him into the wilds of New York. Often in a rather hard-nosed way, the 'seventies cop movies reflect current concern with the problems of the cities or at least with the violence

Two sorts of professional in *The New Centurions*, with (*below*) Stacy Keach and George C. Scott.

which is their most widely recognised symptom. In the company of Eastwood in *Dirty Harry* and George C. Scott in *The New Centurions*, we are shown the jungle from the viewpoint of its denizens. Detective Harry Callaghan seems always to be coming upon some violent criminal enterprise – it seems that he has only to go for a quick hamburger to get caught up in stopping a bank robbery (in *Dirty Harry*) or an aeroplane hijacking (in *Magnum Force*). The rich texture of city life revealed in *The New Centurions* includes baby battering, stick-ups and sudden, pointless killing. These films (and their rural counterparts, *Electra Glide in Blue* and *Walking Tall*) share an episodic structure which seems expressly designed to offer something of a sampler of society's ills.

In the 'seventies police movies, violence is presented (and often stressed) as a fact. Indeed, apart from the implication that there is a lot of it around, the nearest thing to a point these movies make about violence is its pointlessness – both *The New Centurions* and *Electra Glide in Blue* end with the completely gratuitous deaths of the heroes. This assumption of violence as a fact of life within the setting of the films has not helped endear them to the critics who expect cinematic violence to be deployed sparingly and only where justified by moral impact or thematic necessity. Otherwise, violence is condemned as excessive; the naughty word 'exploitation' is invoked. One can equally argue, though, that anything less than direct presentation of violence and its effects (which often offend the critics more than the violence itself) is dangerous in presenting the idea of violence divorced from the unpleasantness of its results – one should discount the often-repeated critical misapprehension that such things can be implied more powerfully than they can be shown. Anyone who still believes that might do well to watch, say, the beating up of Marlon Brando in Arthur Penn's *The Chase* (1965) which is more painful to the audience than one can imagine any discreetly implied version would be.

In the escalation from the bloodless blasting of the 'thirties to the casually extreme violence of the 'seventies, the middle and late 'fifties produced one development that proved to be something of a dead end: an almost decorative use of violence, which in its way might be seen as representing a sort of decadence of the established forms of gangster movie. Joseph H. Lewis's *The Big Combo* (1954) had torture by turning up the volume of a hearing-aid and yelling into it. Rudolph Maté's *Second Chance* (1953) included Linda Darnell stabbing Jack Palance through the hand with an old-fashioned steel-nibbed pen. Fritz Lang's *The Big Heat* (1953) had Lee Marvin disfiguring Gloria Grahame by throwing the contents of a Cona flask of boiling coffee in her face. The great film, though, for violence as embellishment is Robert Aldrich's film of Mickey Spillane's *Kiss Me, Deadly* (1955): Mike Hammer (Ralph Meeker) inflicts torture by crushing fingers in a desk drawer and – more spiritually –

An ingenious way of heightening a scene of violence in *Killer's Kiss*.

by snapping one of an opera-lover's treasured Caruso 78s before his eyes; Hammer's motor-mechanic friend Nick Dennis is crushed to death when Hammer's jacked-up car, on which he is working, is let down on him. The taste for offbeat violence even spread abroad; in France, Edouard Molinaro's *Des femmes disparaissent* (1958) uses an extending car radio aerial as a conveniently portable instrument for chastisement. Nicholas Ray's *Party Girl* (1948), which Lawrence Alloway describes as 'one of the first feature films to specify impact and wounds with a new abundance of blood', is also full of recherché allusions to violence: Lee J. Cobb pouring vitriol on a paper Christmas decoration to demonstrate to Robert Taylor what it would do to Cyd Charisse.

The cinematic route by which the new scale of violence came to the American screen is not too difficult to plot. One can go back to 1954 and the Japanese film, *The Seven Samurai*, directed by Akira Kurosawa, who was an admirer of John Ford and gave to his Oriental story something of Ford's feeling for action – westernised it, even. The film's international success inspired a half-baked though very popular western remake, John Sturges's *The Magnificent Seven* (1960), but in Japan also started the samurai action movie as a genre which grew increasingly violent. The spare-

Ralph Meeker looks at Fortunio Bonanova's records in *Kiss Me, Deadly*.

Opposite: after the sheriff has been beaten up in *The Chase,* with Marlon Brando and Angie Dickinson.

77

Inger Stevens drops the piece of broken glass which she has used to stab Neville Brand in *Cry Terror*.

Bonnie and Clyde with Faye Dunaway, Warren Beatty and (*below*) Michael J. Pollard.

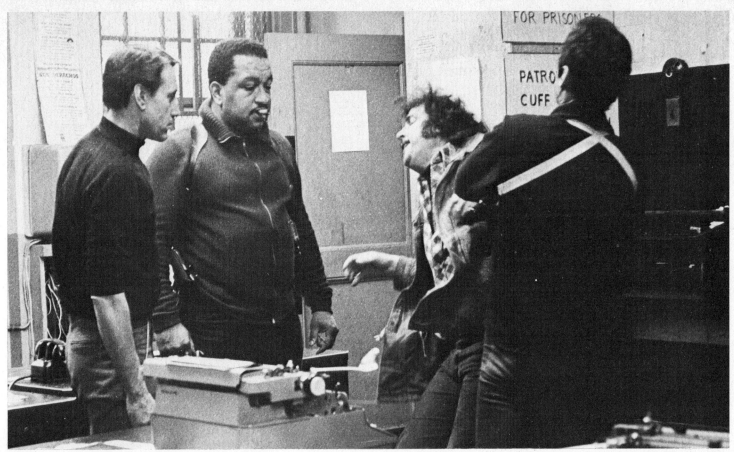

part surgery to transplant the violence (plus some less compatible elements of samurai posturing) into the western was accomplished by Sergio Leone in Italy with *A Handful of Dollars* (1964) and its successors. These films did not reach the English-language market immediately, but by 1968 follow-up movies were starting to be made in America, though it took Sam Peckinpah's *The Wild Bunch* in the following year to establish large-scale western bloodletting as a homegrown product. In other genres, violence had started to be portrayed with increasing directness, for example by Cornel Wilde in *Lancelot and Guinevere* (1962) and *The Naked Prey* (1966), a jungle movie. In general, though, the new level of stated violence seems to have been stimulated by the arrival of the Clint Eastwood westerns.

A more direct trigger to violence in American movies came from an unrelated source, Arthur Penn's *Bonnie and Clyde*, which was premièred in August 1967, three months after the American release of the second Clint Eastwood western. Like many very successful movies, it was released with little promotional effort by the studio. It gained a lot of publicity by being written up as symptomatic of current violence, particularly in 1968, which was the year of the Martin Luther King and Robert Kennedy assassinations. It was attacked by pundits such as Arthur Schlesinger Jr, who identified 'its blithe acceptance of the world of violence – an acceptance which almost became a celebration'.

This may be a rather overwrought reaction, but, as Robin Wood points out in his book on Penn, 'The Bonnie and Clyde of Penn's film, however many banks they rob, however many

Some questioning in *The Seven-Ups* with Roy Scheider.

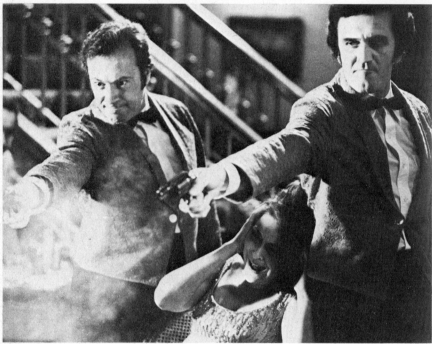

Above: The Don Is Dead.
Right: Honor Thy Father.

Opposite: Kim Darby as Miss Blandish sees her boy friend (Alex Wilson) fatally shot in *The Grissom Gang.*

men they kill, remain attractive and sympathetic characters: plainly, the most attractive and sympathetic in the film. Obviously, the intense identification audiences feel with the characters is a major factor – *the* major factor in the film's immense box-office success. . . .' But this does not amount to 'blithe acceptance' on the part of the film, for, as Wood notes, 'The process whereby we are made to confront and live through the full implications of the total irresponsibility we have so happily surrendered to is calculated with great exactness; though one scarcely thinks of calculation while watching a film that flows so freely. From the reckless gaiety of the first robbery, each act of violence is made to convey a slightly intenser charge of doubt, anxiety, and finally revulsion.'

The violence in *Bonnie and Clyde* is used as carefully as it was in Penn's earlier (and very different) film, *The Chase*, as an essential element in the director's conception. Both films would be greatly weakened by any curtailment of their violence – in particular, *Bonnie and*

Clyde without its painful depiction of wounds would have come near to justifying Schlesinger's attack. The use of violence is not at all that of the 'seventies urban jungle movies where it is just a commonplace part of the scene. The violence itself, though, does set the scene for later movies in its clear specification of injuries. When John Trevelyan was Secretary of the British Board of Film Censors, one of his great concerns was with the possibility of setting precedents: each rude word, each blow, each nipple that got through, albeit justifiably and in an impeccably serious movie, was likely to undermine his chances of stopping rude words, blows and nipples flooding into less worthy movies. Seen in this light, *Bonnie and Clyde* becomes a key precedent for later movies which are related to it only in the detailing of the violence, not in its impact on the audience.

In the final images of *Bonnie and Clyde*, slow motion is used to show the couple being riddled with bullets. As a specific effect in its particular context, it works, though perhaps rather self-

80

consciously. With the appearance of *The Wild Bunch* (1969), slow motion began to be used indiscriminately for violence. This treatment, which makes much of those pretty parabolas of arterial blood that follow bullet impact in Peckinpah's movie, can be traced back to the samurai movies of the early 'sixties, which sometimes surprised western audiences by doing graceful things with the release of blood or entrails from the losers in sword fights. The curious effect of slow motion on wounding and death in westerns and crime movies is a dissipation of impact – the technique heightens nothing in the action except a certain balletic quality which is usually quite inappropriate. While it may give us more time to savour the carnage, the physical facts become less important than the physical interpretation placed upon them. In a much less interesting way than in the 'fifties, we are again seeing violence used as decoration.

Opposite: The New Centurions.

Exploded car from The Godfather.

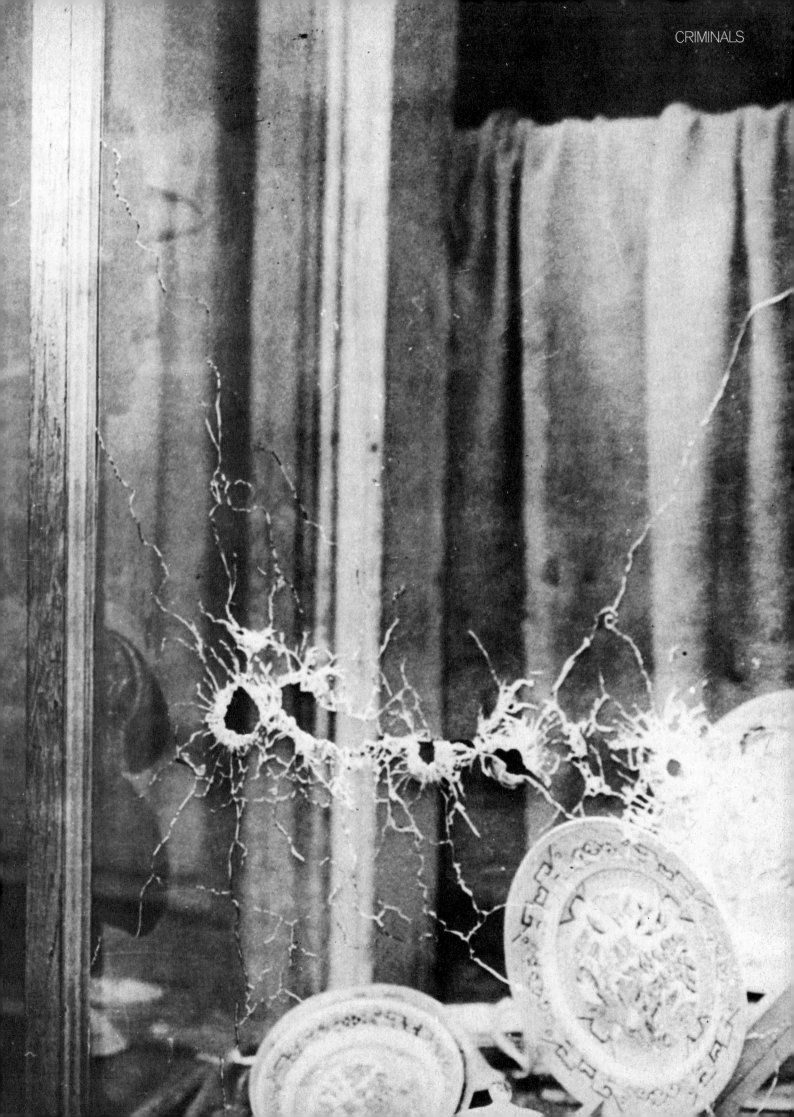

CRIMINALS

In Archie Mayo's *Doorway to Hell* (1930), Lew
Ayres as Louis Ricarno, the Napoleon of the
Underworld, takes his new wife in a chauffeur-
driven limousine to see the slum where he was
born and where his sister and one of his brothers
died of typhoid. This look into the past goes
further towards offering explanations for criminality than was usual soon afterwards when
the gangster cycle got under way. But then,
Doorway to Hell was very much more sophisticated than most of its successors. It took
elements from gangster lore, notably the
brutality of the killings and the idea of organisation above gang level, and used them with
some directness. However, it allied these to a
strong and inventive story-line. Its elegant,
articulate hero organises the city's gangs by
installing himself as overlord, then retires to
write his memoirs. Among the reading matter
that we can see around him is a leather-bound
'Oeuvres de Bossuet'. Seventeenth-century
religious discourses may seem rather outré
literature to appeal to even a recently bereaved
gangster (and raise tantalising questions of
whether the book was planted with intent by,
say, the director or was simply a nice-looking
volume that the property department happened to have). The idea of the book-reading
gangster turns up again in Paul Wendkos's
Honor Thy Father (1973), in which the Bonnano
family's trusted lieutenant reads Sartre's
'Being and Nothingness'. The thought that
gangsters might not be entirely illiterate is not
a purely fictional conceit – in the early part of
1972, Crazy Joe Gallo briefly charmed the upper
crust of New York literati with his references
to Camus and Sartre; his promise as a man of
letters was abruptly terminated by gunfire in an

Italian restaurant on 7 April 1972.

Louis Ricarno in *Doorway to Hell*, who believes that 'war is the greatest racket' and keeps his kid brother in military academy, is an exotic creature compared to the archetypal gangster film protagonist, Caesar Enrico Bandello, Little Caesar. Less than wholehearted commitment to crime tended to become the preserve of those lower in the gangster pecking order – people who have become involved through weakness or force of circumstance. Rico Bandello shares his vision of success with his buddy Joe (Douglas Fairbanks Jr) who turns out to have slightly different ideas: 'Yeah, there's money in the big town alright. And the women. . . . Good times, something doing all the time. Excitement, you know. Say, the clothes I could wear. And then I'd quit, Rico. I'd go back to dancing like I used to before I met you. I don't

James Cagney as the
gangster in Ruth Etting's life
in Love Me or Leave Me,
with Harry Bellaver and
Robert Keith.

know, I ain't mixed for this sort of thing. Dancing, that's what I want to do.' Rico, on the other hand, is figuring on making other people dance. In spite of one minor gunshot wound and a distinct lack of moral fibre, Joe survives to be a successful dancer – the poster hoarding through which Rico is shot advertises Joe and his partner Olga at the Grand Theatre.

We do not learn very much about the protagonist of *Little Caesar*. He is conceited, defiant, fearless, but all these qualities are subordinated to his overriding characteristic, ambition. We know more about Joe than we do about Rico – we are not told what Rico did before the gas-station stick-up which opens the movie. He has no past, no relatives and no relationships which do not involve the execution of crimes or his rise from the ranks of gangland. He exists purely as a gangster, and the film relies for its effectiveness on the extent to which Edward G. Robinson manages to embody on the screen the features and personality of a representative gangster who would be recognised as such by the public of the time. The casting of Robinson is the crucial success in what is otherwise a relatively undistinguished piece of film-making. It is possible that the very lack of any directorial aspirations beyond flatly functional competence worked in the film's favour by adding to the impression of unvarnished documentary truth.

Just as Robinson/Rico fitted the public's conception of a successful gangster in a way that the apparently more glamorous Ayres/Ricarno did not, *Little Caesar* rather than *Doorway to Hell* was the film to set the gangster cycle going. It laid down the groundwork for a decade of future movies and was striking precisely for its simplicity, for the fact that the outlines of the gangster narrative were not complicated as in

Doorway to Hell by other considerations (*Doorway to Hell* could be remade as a western with almost no change in the plot-line). Above all, *Little Caesar* related clearly to some of the more sensational events of the period and to an unsavoury and therefore fascinating side of American life.

The relationship, however, was not a direct one of reportage or documentary reconstruction – Rico, like Tom Powers (James Cagney) in *Public Enemy* and Tony Camonte (Paul Muni) in *Scarface*, is not a screen portrait of an actual gangster but a fictional creation embodying characteristics taken from life, though not from a single villain. Clearly, the main source for Rico is Al Capone, ethnically, in general

Barbra Streisand as Fanny
Brice in Funny Girl.

John Gavin and Lana Turner in *Imitation of Life*.

flamboyant New York cousins. From Chicago come the spectacular funeral of the murdered hood, Tony, attended reverently by his killers, and the shooting in broad daylight on a shopping street. The differences between Rico and Capone are also striking: in status Little Caesar does not rival Al Capone who inherited an army of 700 when Johnny Torrio pulled out from controlling Chicago crime in 1925. The story, too, is largely unconnected with Capone whose connections with Torrio dated from his childhood in Brooklyn and whose conviction happened some months after the release of the film, which ends with the death of the now down-and-out Rico. The rise and fall plot-line of *Little Caesar* laid out one of the standard gangster-movie patterns which continued right through to the nostalgia cycle of the 'sixties.

The presence of Capone, even somewhat transmuted, in Rico might well have been the trick that turned *Little Caesar* into a landmark in film history, for Capone had in the previous two or three years established himself in the public eye as *the* gangster, a position from which downfall and death have not dislodged him; such figures as Lucky Luciano and Meyer Lansky may have become vastly more powerful, but they were also very much more discreet. (A Luciano equivalent did turn up after Lucky's trial and conviction, as Johnny Vanning – played by Eduardo Ciannelli – in *Marked Woman* (1937), a film directly inspired by the predicament of the girls who were witnesses against Luciano.) Capone figures can be found

appearance and in the extent to which he relishes the rewards of his position – he tells Joe that the decorations of his apartment cost 20,000 bucks and offers him 'a cocktail or a dash of brandy' (a phrase we have earlier heard from the lips of The Big Boy, the city's ultimate crime boss); Rico is conscious of his status and poses for the press photographers who turn up at his testimonial banquet – a scene from which the more experienced Diamond Pete Montana discreetly absents himself. The patterns of behaviour, too, are clearly inspired by those of Chicago mobs rather than by those of their less

Paul Muni as Tony Camonte in *Scarface*.

90

in movies from *Scarface* (1932) to *Party Girl* (1958), in which Lee J. Cobb's Rico Angelo exhibits Capone-like fits of violence, beating a faithless henchman to death with a presentation mace at a testimonial dinner; he is also said to be suffering from incipient general paralysis – the cause of Capone's death in 1947. Again Rico Angelo does not appear to be purely Capone inspired – he has an obsession with Jean Harlow, which he shares with at least one real gangster, Abner 'Longie' Zwillman, the boss of the Syndicate in New Jersey, though his is expressed by shooting holes in a portrait of the blonde bombshell because she has got married; Zwillman was said to have attempted to buy pubic hair supposed to have been cut off when the lady had an emergency operation for the removal of her appendix.

But then, as two sources of notoriety, crime and showbiz have often shown a mutual fascination which has sometimes blossomed into courtship. The relationship has not been restricted to the basic level of crime being used as a source of dramatic inspiration with proven public appeal. It takes little entrepreneurial skill to see that a source of hot stories might also provide some saleable performers, particularly where their presence might add a salty whiff of authenticity to the proceedings. Thus Evelyn Nesbit, a chorus girl who was in-

Above and left: John Dall and Peggy Cummins in a fictionalised Bonnie and Clyde story, Joseph H. Lewis's *Gun Crazy* (known in Britain as *Deadly Is The Female*, 1949).

Paul Muni in *Scarface* with Ann Dvorak (*above*), Karen Morley and Osgood Perkins (*below*).

volved in a particularly celebrated high society *crime passionnel*, reappeared on stage as a seaside vaudeville attraction (a sad story that was memorably retold in Richard Fleischer's *The Girl in the Red Velvet Swing*). John Dillinger Sr and Evelyn Frechette, respectively father and mistress of the defunct Public Enemy No. 1,

made stage appearances in the mid 'thirties with other members of the Dillinger family. (John H. Dillinger himself had been gunned down by Federal agents as he emerged from seeing a movie, W.S. Van Dyke's *Manhattan Melodrama*.) It was even possible to use a good dose of reflected notoriety as a stepping-stone to more respectable shows: Dale Winter, a widow after only three weeks of marriage to the Chicago crime boss Big Jim Colosimo, was starring on Broadway within a month of her husband's demise. Later, violent death also brought new magic to the career of one established star. The knifing of one of Lana Turner's later husbands, Johnny Stompinato, by her daughter was followed by one of her greatest successes, Douglas Sirk's *Imitation of Life*, which was about a mother and daughter in love with the same man.

A frequent point of contact between crime and the performing arts was in personal relationships. Somewhere in the iconography of showbusiness there lurks a not unjustified idea that follies girls and starlets are natural companions for the criminal classes. Such interdisciplinary relationships have emerged into the authenticating scrutiny of the public eye usually when one or other partner has had star quality: Big Jim Colosimo and Dale Winter or, on the other hand, the public private lives of Ruth Etting and Fanny Brice – both grist for later musicals, respectively *Love Me or Leave Me* and *Funny Girl*. Where both partners were in the big time, the story was usually kept down to the level of rumour, such as the names of Benjamin 'Bugsy' Siegel's Hollywood girl friends apart from his regular, Virginia Hill, in whose Beverly Hills home he was finally rubbed out in 1947. Late 'thirties Hollywood had been fascinated by Siegel, one of the founding fathers of the Bug and Meyer Mob, the predecessor of Murder Inc., who had arrived after the signs of decay in a five-year-old alibi had made it wise for him to leave New York. Although he was on the West Coast to extend Syndicate operations to Southern California, his life as a celebrity foreshadowed Joe Gallo's brief period as a fashionable guest in 1971 New York, with the exception that Siegel was shaking down the very stars who were socialising with him: in one year, he collected $400,000 from them in loans which operated on a strictly one-way basis.

The movies, though, were more than just a source of revenue for the criminals. A report in 'Variety' has lately recalled memories from the 'thirties of gangsters queuing for opening-day matinées of new crime movies on Broadway to be the first to pick up any new ruses devised as fiction by ingenious screenwriters. Ben Hecht's autobiography mentions a visit from Al Capone's representatives who had got wind of the making of *Scarface* – this early piece of PR consciousness is transmuted in Joseph M. Newman's *The George Raft Story* (1961) into a direct confrontation between Raft and Capone (who would by that time have been safely in prison).

In the flood of publicity which attended successes in both lines of business, movies and crime had to be well informed about each other. The plethora of material to be found in the press could hardly have been ignored by screenwriters as free source material: both the characters and the incidents for their screenplays were there for the taking. However, for all manner of reasons apart from the niceties of narrative construction, actuality had to be processed with changes of location, context or personnel before it could appear re-enacted in a gangster movie. The depiction of real gangsters successfully executing real crimes would not have been allowed by the newly established Hays Office, which would certainly have refused to let straight biographies of notorious contemporary criminals be offered as family entertainment. In any case, a minimum condition would have been a rewrite of life's scenario to provide terminal retribution every time

So Rico Bandello in *Little Caesar* isn't exactly Capone, and nor is Tony Camonte in *Scarface*, but both are clearly derived from Capone and must have depended for some of their appeal on the public identifying Capone through the camouflage of fictionalisation. Indeed, the use of Capone's nickname as the title of *Scarface* was about as far as it was possible to go in hint-

Edward G. Robinson and Humphrey Bogart in *Bullets or Ballots*.

Jack Lambert, Ralph Meeker and Jack Elam in *Kiss Me, Deadly*.

ing at the protagonist's real equivalent. It was not until the mid 'forties that gangster films began to be made using actual names, and by that time the events shown were a decade in the past; more than that, the intervening war must have made their subjects seem part of a bygone era. When they appeared, they were not major studio productions like the early 'thirties crime movies but such B-features and Poverty Row efforts as *Machine Gun Mama* and *Roger Touhy, Gangster* (both 1944) and *Dillinger* (1945), a cheapie starring Lawrence Tierney, which used the bank-robbery footage from Fritz Lang's *You Only Live Once* (1937). It is notable that this first clutch of gangster biographies dealt with small independent gangs rather than with organised crime – it was not until the beginning of the nostalgia cycle that a big-time mobster was portrayed in a straight biography, and the subject was inevitable: it was *Al Capone* (1959). Real names, though, were mentioned rather earlier – Fritz Lang's *The Big Heat* (1953), made after the Kefauver Committee hearings of 1950–51, does mention Lucky Luciano by name.

Real incidents also turn up, suitably modified, in the 'thirties gangster movies. Thus, the big shoot-out between the Feds and Barton McLane's mob round a shooting-lodge in

'G' Men (1935) was clearly inspired by the FBI's
largely abortive operation against a group
including Dillinger and Lester Gillis (alias
Baby Face Nelson) at the Little Bohemia Lodge
roadhouse near Mercer, Wisconsin, on 22 April
1934, although many of the circumstances were
changed in the film. The exercise of drawing
such parallels could be pursued with diminish-
ing returns through film after film. A very
different example, though, is mentioned by the
crime reporter Hank Messick: Nails Morton,
winner of a Croix de Guerre but also a member
of Dion O'Banion's gang in Chicago, learned to
ride at the Colorado ranch of a colleague,
Cowboy Alterie. 'Upon returning to Chicago,
he was thrown from a horse in Lincoln Park
and kicked to death. O'Banion led a firing
squad to the stables and took the horse for a
walk. The execution was celebrated at a wild
party and was immortalised in the movie,
Public Enemy. . . .'

Quite apart from being of note in dealing with
non-Latin gangsters, this picture also features
a strikingly inept performance by Jean Harlow.
As her relationship is with the protagonist,
James Cagney, her presence is an obvious first
stage towards a more elaborate treatment of
the star gangster. Perhaps *Little Caesar* was the
sole archetype of the genre, unique among A-
features in the extent to which it is purely a
gangster movie. Only Glenda Farrell as Olga is
extraneous to the world of crime – all the other
main characters are gangsters, their associates and the police – and her main function is
to give Joe (Douglas Fairbanks Jr) some determination to break with Rico. It was inevitable
that the starkly rudimentary outlines of *Little
Caesar* would need to be elaborated in later
movies to retain everyone's interest. Thus
Howard Hawks talking to Peter Bogdanovich:
'*Scarface* was really the story of Al Capone.
When I asked Ben Hecht to write it, he said,
"Oh, we don't want to do a gangster picture."
And I said, "Well, this is a little different. I
would like to do the Capone family as if they
were the Borgias set down in Chicago." And he

95

said, "We'll start tomorrow." We took eleven
days to write the story and dialogue. We were
influenced a good deal by the incestuous elements in the story of the Borgias. We made the
brother-sister relationship clearly incestuous.
But the censors misunderstood our intention
and objected to it because they thought the
relationship was too beautiful to be attributed
to a gangster. . . .'

Although the Hays Office missed out on the
incest, the story does indicate the problems in
giving gangsters any positive characteristics
of the sort which would reinforce their appeal
to audiences – unmitigated rat offers very little
mileage as a movie hero. Even Rico Bandello
showed an embryonic plus side in his feelings
of duty towards Joe, although otherwise he
could only be admired for his ambition and
drive. Some degree of love interest was a useful
addition to the gangster character, but there
were clearly limits within which it could be

portrayed.

One very serviceable way of demonstrating
that some lawbreaker has fine human qualities
of one sort or another is to provide as contrast
a villain who is conspicuously devoid of a single
decent instinct. Early versions of this can be
seen in William Keighley's police movies of the
mid 'thirties. In 'G' Men, there is Barton
McLane as the really bad bad guy and there is
William Harrigan who has spent $20,000 getting
James Cagney an education and putting him
through law school: 'I've been in the rackets
all my life and it doesn't pay anything except
money.' Bullets or Ballots has McLane as the
boss gangster who is extrovert and boastful but
not vicious, which Humphrey Bogart as his
lieutenant, Bugs Fenner, definitely is.

Three years later, Bogart elaborated on the

Bugs Fenner character in that of George Hally
in Raoul Walsh's The Roaring Twenties, this
time as contrast for the good bootlegger, Eddie
Bartlett, played by James Cagney. Very early
in our acquaintance with George, he is display-
ing his brutal sense of humour on the battle-
fields of France: one of his comrades refrains
from shooting a German soldier when he sees
that the enemy is a kid about fifteen years old.
George aims his rifle offscreen towards the
German and shoots, remarking, 'He'll never
be sixteen.' Later, in partnership with Eddie
emptying a government warehouse of confiscated liquor, George takes pleasure in killing
his sergeant from the army who is now working
as a guard. Like many of the more vicious film
villains, George is ultimately cowardly – in the
final confrontation, he finds himself at the

wrong end of a gun wielded by a dishevelled, alcoholic Eddie. Before his demise, he provides a fine display of cringing: 'You always was a fair guy, Eddie.'

The juxtaposition of good gangster and bad gangster continued through the fall-guy cycle of the late 'forties: for every potentially decent ex-con like Burt Lancaster in *Criss Cross*, there is likely to be an entirely unscrupulous Dan Duryea ready to lure him back into crime with every intention of setting him up to take the rap. In the 'fifties, there were a number of actors who specialised in such thorough nastiness that their mere presence in a movie was virtually an extenuating circumstance for the leading heavy – among the more memorable were Lyle Bettger, Jack Lambert and Myron Healey. Their espousal of a life of crime seems only to be expected; it is when nice guys take to operating outside the law that explanations are needed.

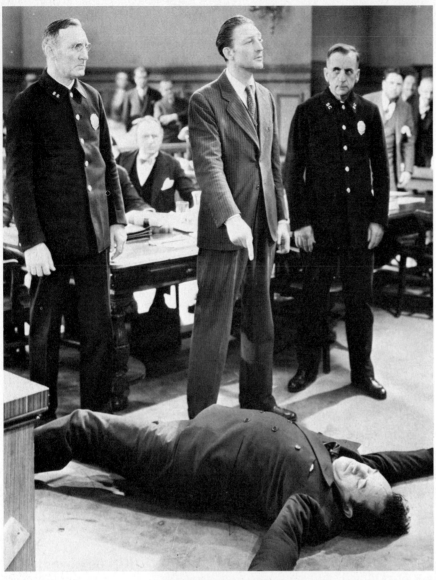

Warren William conducts a dramatic defence in *The Mouthpiece*.

The background to *The Roaring Twenties* was a post-New Deal willingness to recognise the social ills of the nation so that they might be remedied. Hollywood's involvement in this feeling (which was to bring it trouble from the House Committee on Un-American Activities) produced, among other things, films dealing with childhood in slum conditions: William Wyler's *Dead End* (1937) and Michael Curtiz's *Angels with Dirty Faces* (1938), both with Bogart, the latter also with Cagney. *The Roaring Twenties* complements these indications of the social roots of crime with a historical treatment, and places great emphasis on its authenticity. The credits are followed by a foreword from Mark Hellinger, the author of the story, who had been a reporter on the New York 'Daily News' in the 'twenties and a columnist on the New York 'Daily Mirror' from 1930 to 1938. This seasoned and widely syndicated journalist assures the audience in a signed statement that the characters are composites of people he knew and the situations are composites of ones that actually occurred. The story alternates with short documentary sections in the style of American popular journalism as translated to film by *March of Time* (a strikingly urgent approach which has long gone out of fashion – its last notable screen appearance was in Walter Winchell's narration for *The Untouchables* television series). Thus the film is given a topical prologue about the beginnings of the Second World War before going back to 'April 1918 – almost a million young men are engaged in a struggle which they have been told will make the world safe for democracy.'

A second documentary section takes us to late 1919 and the last American detachments

Ida Lupino and Humphrey Bogart in *High Sierra*.

coming back from policing the Rhine. Eddie gets back to find that his job as a garage mechanic has been taken by someone else. The montage sequence on post-war unemployment embodies a feeling of the disillusionment of soldiers returning to 'the same old struggle, the struggle to survive'. Eddie's friend Danny (Frank McHugh) suggests they split the time on his taxi-cab which he uses for only twelve hours a day. The next sequence of newsreel material documents the start of the Volstead Act and tells us that the forces of the underworld were moving in on the liquor business.

Eddie in his cab delivers a package to a speakeasy and gets arrested together with the joint's owner Panama Smith (Gladys George) for handling illegal liquor. 'I know a lawyer,' he tells her. 'It would be better if you knew a judge.' Because he helps her beat the rap, she pays his $100 fine, saving him from sixty days in jail. She thinks he's a pretty decent guy, and decent guys are hard to find. Back with Panama in the speak, he witnesses an exemplary scene of police helpfulness: a cop comes in to look for a man who has parked his car in front of a hydrant. So Eddie becomes 'part of an army' of lawbreakers, the product of 'an unpopular law and an unwilling public'. Another montage shows us some of the more grotesque aspects of illegal liquor consumption including the undertaking parlour as a front. Then we are shown Eddie being given the bad news that there has been a price increase of a dollar a bottle. But he says that he can make this tiger sweat himself – he's got a bath-tub too. Eddie blending spirits in his bath is followed by a scene of customer reaction: 'This is the real stuff – you can't fool me.'

Once Eddie has made it as a bootlegger, manufacturing his own product and running a fleet of taxis to deliver it, he sees no reason to stop: 'While the gravy's flowing, I want to have my kisser right there under the faucet.' The only person who has reservations is his lawyer, Lloyd (Jeffrey Lynn), a friend from the war – the man who declined to shoot the fifteen-year-old German. Once Eddie has started breaking the law, a process facilitated by the Volstead Act, natural ambition moves him towards bigger things. Refused supplies of better-quality liquor by a man who actually imports the stuff, he and his men masquerade as coast-

guards to hijack the boat which is bringing it in. Running the import operation is George who readily agrees to go into partnership – he has the organisation to get it and bring it in and Eddie has the organisation to peddle it.

Another burst of documentary montage introduces us to 1924, to increasing violence and organised crime and to a new and deadly weapon, the tommy. Now murder could be parcelled out in wholesale lots. The montage leads into the robbery of the government warehouse which Eddie and George have made sure is well stocked by the simple expedient of tipping off the cops about a consignment being brought in by George's former employer: 'The government takes it from Nick Brown, and we take it from the government – very neat.'

But George is not the man to be satisfied with being in partnership. When Eddie sets about organising the other bootleggers, George sends Eddie's friend Danny to fetch Nick Brown, who is still apparently resentful as he returns Danny's body with a note in the pocket saying 'You leave me alone and I'll leave you alone.' George declines to go on a raid to even the score and instead tips off Brown. In the end, though, it is not just George but history as well that puts Eddie out of the bootlegging business.

Another montage shows us 1929 – 'Black Tuesday, October 29: more than $16\frac{1}{2}$ million dollars are knocked off the price of shares in a single day.' In a sudden plunge into expressionism, we are shown the buildings of Wall

Left: Ida Lupino at the end of *High Sierra*.

George Raft and Humphrey Bogart in *Invisible Stripes*.

99

Victor Mature and Richard Conte in *Criss Cross*.

Sam Jaffe, Jean Hagen and Sterling Hayden in *The Asphalt Jungle*.

Street melting away. Eddie is told by his broker that he needs $200,000 straight away or he'll have to sell him out. So Eddie attempts to raise the money by selling 40 per cent of his share of the bootlegging operation to George, who has an alternative proposition: $250,000 for the lot, and he'll also leave Eddie one cab.

The last of the montage sequences offers an optimistic gloss (though one which would have been widely accepted when the film was made) on the events of the early 'thirties. The Depression, we are told, caused liquor profits to collapse – the bootleggers became unable to pay protection. Newsreels take us up to the end of Prohibition. But far from being undermined by the Depression and closed down by the repeal of the Volstead Act, the villains were doing better than ever. As Hank Messick puts it, 'early in 1933 . . . those banks that had survived now locked their doors. The only people left with money, so went the bitter joke, were the bootleggers. This was the most important

moment in the history of organised crime. For the bootleggers did have cash, millions times millions of dollars, and it was stashed away in shoeboxes hidden under beds, in wall safes, in clothes closets, in cans buried in back yards. It was, in other words, liquid.' With the advantage of having cash when no one legitimate had any to spare, organised crime was able to implant itself firmly into big business, especially, says Messick, 'those industries having a cash flow like the movies or those catering to basic human needs like restaurants, clothing manufacturers, grocery stores'. And even after the repeal of Prohibition, illicit liquor remained important as it was tax free and could be sold at a huge profit for half the price of the legal stuff. Such was the scale of these operations that one of the Syndicate's chain of illegal distilleries, at Zanesville, Ohio, was at the time said to be the largest in the world (the plant could make 5,000 gallons of hundred proof a day and five times that volume of beer).

The one person in *The Roaring Twenties* who has not yet been mentioned here, even though she has billing above the main title with Cagney rather than below it with Bogart, is Priscilla Lane, as Jean Sherman, who appears in the war sequence as a sultry photograph which she has sent with a letter. But when Eddie goes to visit his pen-friend in Minneola, Long Island, he finds that she is a sailor-suited schoolgirl whose picture was taken when she was in the high school play – 'The Gipsy Fortune Teller' by Victor Herbert. She next appears in the chorus line of a Broadway musical where Cagney has gone backstage to collect a bootlegging debt. He gets her a job singing at Panama's speakeasy and falls in love with her. She, however, has fallen for the lawyer, Lloyd. A sidewalk confrontation peters out after Eddie has socked Lloyd only once before accepting the situation and going off to sample his own booze.

The denouement starts with Jean getting into a cab which turns out to have Eddie driving. He takes her home and meets Lloyd who is now with the District Attorney's office. The days of the rackets, says Lloyd, are over. A threat delivered to Jean by some ugly-looking henchmen that Lloyd should bury what the DA's office has on George or they'll bury him sends Jean looking for help from Eddie. She traces him to a bar where Panama is working as an off-key canary and Eddie is hitting the bottle. Although he gives Jean a hard time when she asks him to talk to George, he is persuaded by Panama's argument that he's got to do something for them as they have something to look forward to. The henchmen let Eddie in 'to give the boss a laugh' but the visit ends with George dead and Eddie being shot down by George's men. Eddie collapses and dies on the steps of a church as Panama arrives and is asked by a cop who he is. 'This is Eddie Bartlett.' 'How are you hooked up with him?' 'I could never figure it out.' 'Well, what was his business?' 'He used to be a big shot.'

Jean Gabin in *Le Jour se lève* (*left*) and Henry Fonda in the remake, *The Long Night* (*above*).

Richard Widmark as Tommy Udo takes Victor Mature as Nick Bianco to a high-class brothel in *Kiss of Death*.

Jack Palance as the carrier of bubonic plague in Elia Kazan's *Panic in the Streets* (1950).

James Cagney as Cody Jarrett, stricken with a fit, and Margaret Wycherley as Ma Jarrett in *White Heat*.

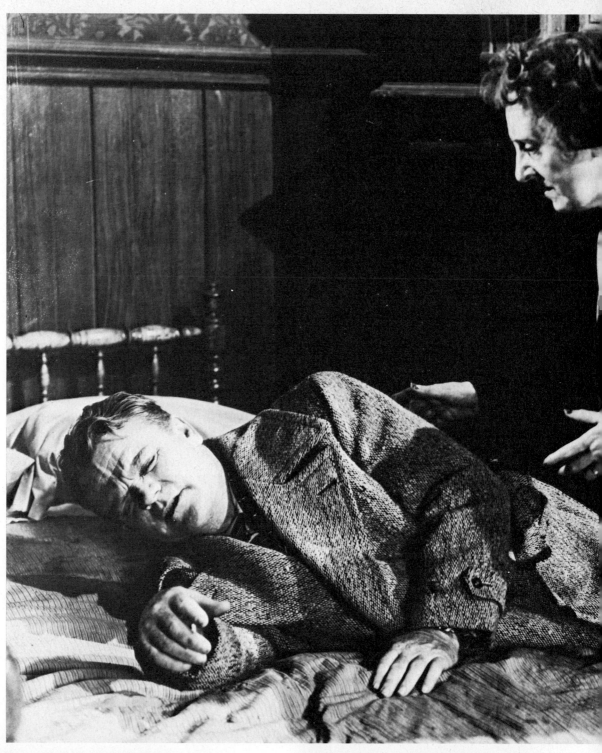

Below: White Heat. James Cagney with Edmond O'Brien and Virginia Mayo (*left*) and with Steve Cochran and steam-scalded colleague in the opening train robbery.

has gone up and that his employer is unwilling to sack the man who has been doing his job in his absence. This treatment continues throughout the film so that we are kept aware of the larger forces that bear on the crucial phases of his career. While sometimes, as in the section on post-war unemployment, Eddie's situation is treated as being representative of a general problem, he is never depicted as the helpless victim of historical circumstance – this would reduce him to a puppet figure and the film to purely didactic drama, which it certainly is not. Eddie is a free agent and almost defiantly self-reliant; he is clearly free to decide that nothing is more important than respect for the letter of the law. Yet his decisions can hardly help being influenced by external factors – most strikingly, his first steps into the bootlegging business are encouraged by his experience of the operations of the law. There is every reason to believe that only the loss of his job stopped him working steadily and conscientiously as a mechanic; without the foolishness of Prohibition and his brush with the law he could well have gone on being a cab-driver. There is no reason at all, though, to believe that George would, in a more benign world, have been anything other than a moderately vicious criminal.

The sympathetic treatment accorded to

James Cagney in the last sequence of *White Heat*.

The subject of the epitaph, however, could hardly have been further from the criminal big shot represented by any of the cinematic Al Capone equivalents. Eddie has been shown throughout the film as being inherently a nice, straight guy, and this appraisal is maintained even when he is at the height of his power as a big shot – his reaction to the news that Jean is going off to marry Lloyd is entirely normal.

The film's alternation and blending of documentary with fiction firmly places the fictional sequences as specific illustrations of the general, historical developments set out in the documentary passages. Thus we are told about the last soldiers returning from Europe to find a changed and unwelcoming world and then see Eddie coming back to discover that his rent

Eddie, the nice guy who has the misfortune to exemplify the socio-historical roots of crime, allows him to love and be loved (even if not by the same woman). The two relationships, which both tend to increase our valuation of Eddie as a person, are very standard gangster-movie components as are the two ladies involved: Jean, the innocent whom Eddie helps and unrequitedly loves, and the experienced Panama, who is evidently devoted to him but never voices her feelings to him. Although Eddie has to be killed at the end, he is allowed an inherently self-sacrificing and thus heroic death.

The standardness of the basic relationships between Eddie and the two female characters does not detract from the very considerable merit of *The Roaring Twenties* – much more it

103

indicates the skill of Raoul Walsh and the writers in deploying conventional elements in an effective and meaningful way. Thus one is not attacking the film by identifying an example of similar relationships in a much earlier movie, *The Mouthpiece* (1932), directed by James Flood and Elliott Nugent from a play by Frank Collins; the danger in identifying similarities in pattern is that what is generally commonplace in a movie may obscure what is specifically good about it.

In *The Mouthpiece*, the central character is not a gangster but a lawyer from the District Attorney's office (Warren William) whose effi-

Above: Jack Klugman and Angie Dickinson as two of the heavies in *Cry Terror*. *Right and above right:* Frank Sinatra makes his presence felt in *Suddenly*.

Opposite page: Humphrey Bogart in *The Desperate Hours*.

104

John Garfield, Lana Turner and Alan Reed in *The Postman Always Rings Twice*.

Barbara Stanwyck and Fred MacMurray in *Double Indemnity*.

106

cacy as a prosecutor sends an innocent man to
the electric chair. The arrival of this revelation
as the penitentiary lights are dimming leads
him to give up his job and take to the bottle
before surfacing again as an underworld lawyer
and becoming immensely rich. Here the devoted supporter is his secretary (Aline Mac-
Mahon) and the innocent is an inexperienced
typist in his office. He tries to seduce the girl
but is repulsed and develops more spiritual
feelings towards her. When her fiancé, a bank-
messenger, is framed as an accomplice in a
robbery which has been done by one of his
underworld clients, the lawyer is prevailed
upon by his secretary to help, and thus gets
himself shot, leaving the incriminating papers
in the DA's safe. He expires in a cab on the way
to the emergency hospital with his faithful
secretary. 'Good old Hickey, you're always
there when I need you . . . sweetheart . . .' (his
last word is not entirely unequivocal as he has
previously used it in talking to his criminal

associates).

It is not surprising that *The Roaring Twenties*
should echo structures from earlier movies, for
it is in many ways a summing-up of 'thirties
crime movies. Made some years after the other
notable gangster pictures, it has sufficient distance from the events to take the present-tense
treatment of the earlier pictures and place it in
a firmly retrospective, historical framework. In
looking at the causes as well as at the fact of
crime, it is representative of late 'thirties
liberal Hollywood. It was the last movie of any
significance that could look at Prohibition days
as being simply a few years back rather than
part of a different era, which it would be when
seen from the other side of the Second World
War. *The Roaring Twenties* also has a quality
that is much more difficult to pin down but
seems common to many pre-war crime movies:
a chipper resilience – most completely embodied by James Cagney – that prevents even
the sequences when things are going badly for

Joan Crawford and Ann Blyth in *Mildred Pierce*.

the characters from becoming conspicuously neurotic or brooding. In a sense, it is lack of premeditation, but it could also be described as optimism.

Having made the last of the 'thirties crime movies, Raoul Walsh, then in perhaps his finest period as a director, went on a few films later to make the picture that definitively set the style for scores of post-war movies. *High Sierra* was released in January 1941, only fifteen months after *The Roaring Twenties*, but it is an incomparably blacker picture and the antecedent of the fall-guy cycle that dated from the immediate post-war period. It has an intensity that is not merely lacking in the earlier picture but quite alien to it.

Pardoned and released from prison after over eight years, Roy Earle (Humphrey Bogart) goes first to a park to make sure that the grass is still green and the trees are still growing. This briefly lyrical sequence makes us aware of Earle's sensitivity before we learn more about him – the sequence ends with a park-keeper spiking a newspaper which has a headline on the release of Roy Earle, the Indiana Bank Robber. In this line of business, he would thus have been a contemporary of John Dillinger and Baby Face Nelson.

The explanatory background which made up much of *The Roaring Twenties* is almost taken as read. All we are offered is an indication of a past of rural poverty in a visit to his family home, a humble and now more or less derelict weather-boarded structure. In common with many later movies, *High Sierra* is not concerned with how the hero got to be a criminal but with the way he is trapped in this role. Very

William Lundigan and Rhonda Fleming in *Inferno*.

soon after his release, he has the position spelled out to him by the nasty ex-cop Krammer (Barton MacLane): 'Mac spent a fortune springing you – now he calls the tune and you dance to it.' There is no examination here of the difficulties confronting the ex-con in going straight as there was in Lloyd Bacon's *Invisible Stripes* (1939). The availability for Earle of any alternative to a life of crime is never suggested. Where Eddie's decisions in *The Roaring Twenties* are shaped by outside factors, Roy Earle's freedom of action exists only within the limits of his inescapable role as a criminal.

Yet a predominant part of the film's imagery

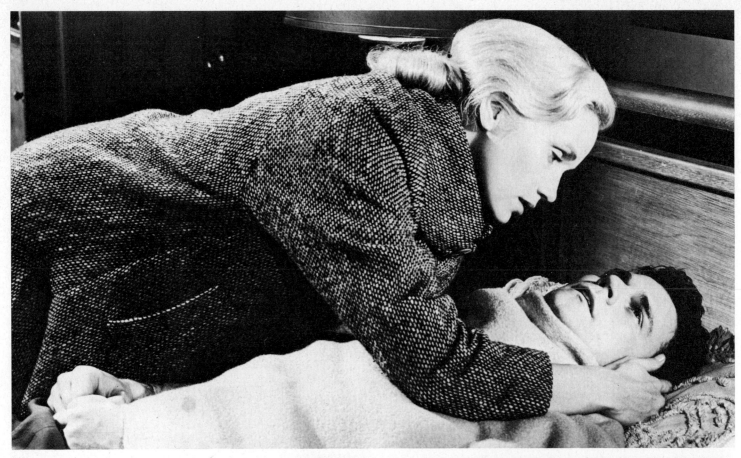

Drug problems. *Above:* Eva Marie Saint and Don Murray in *A Hatful of Rain. Right:* Darren McGavin as the pusher and Frank Sinatra as the junkie in *The Man with the Golden Arm*.

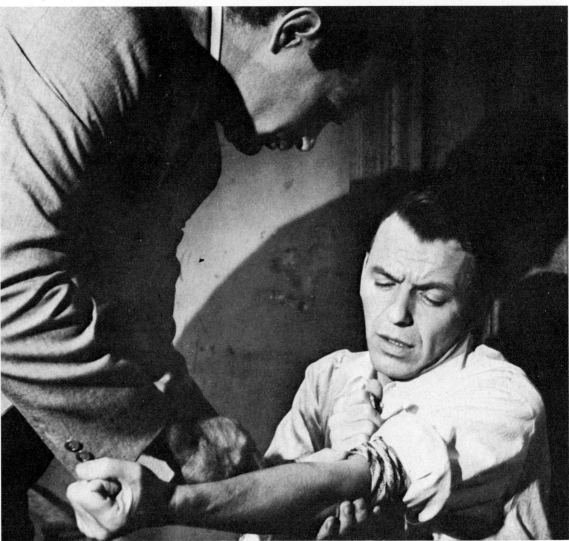

Opposite page. Above: Panic in Needle Park. Below: Bill Hickman as a Narcotics Officer catches a drug smuggler (Eddie Egan) in *The French Connection.*

110

has to do with the idea of freedom. It appears in Roy's dream about crashing out of prison, a dream which could be part memory, part metaphor – we have already learned from him that he was just getting ready for another crash out when his pardon came. Other images of freedom are the stars, about which he talks to Velma (Joan Leslie), and the High Sierras themselves, on which he invites his own death rather than go back to prison. After he has been killed, Marie (Ida Lupino) expresses the idea that now he is free. Death as the only freedom for a criminal is an idea that had already appeared in the rather different emotional context of Fritz Lang's *You Only Live Once* (1937) and was to appear in later movies including *The Asphalt Jungle* (1950) for which the two writers of *High Sierra*, John Huston and W.R. Burnett, were respectively director/joint scriptwriter and author of the original story.

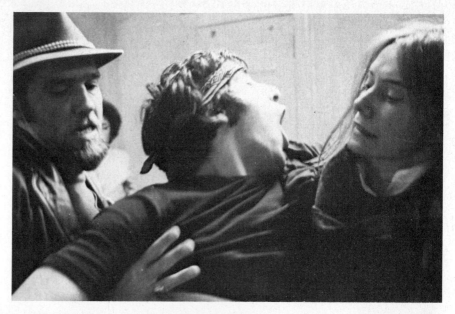

Marlon Brando in *The Wild One*.

The two main female characters in the film are equivalents of Jean and Panama in *The Roaring Twenties*, but the differences are a measure of the change in feeling. Velma is a cripple. The image of her as the total innocent is slightly modified when her father tells Roy that she has a fellow back home, about thirty, divorced and in the insurance business. Nevertheless, Roy falls in love with Velma and also gets an underworld doctor to operate on her foot. 'Oh, Roy,' she cries on hearing the news that it can be fixed, 'you're so good . . . just about the best man that ever lived.' But after the operation has freed her from her affliction, she turns down Roy's proposal of marriage, but says they can still be friends. Her future behaviour, though, is not going to fit Roy's picture of her. She tells her father: 'I'm not

Glenn Ford and Vic Morrow in *Blackboard Jungle*.

crippled any more, Pa. From now on I'm going to have fun. . . .' The last time he visits her, there is a party in progress and it is clear that quite a lot of drink has been consumed. Velma is dancing. The fellow in the insurance business has turned up and offers to pay Roy back the money he has spent on the operation. Roy learns what the audience has realised already – that Velma has never loved him – and leaves disillusioned, his only link with the non-criminal world removed.

Marie occupies a roughly similar position to Panama in the earlier film, but where Panama was the owner of a speakeasy and clearly a lady capable of making her own way, Marie is a slightly pathetic, if determined, floozy who was picked up by Roy's younger partners in a Los Angeles dance hall. After Roy's nightmare, she tells him that she crashed out, too, to the dime and dance joint. Getting away from Los Angeles and taking up with Roy represent two further stages in her escape. But although she goes with him on the hotel robbery, she is on the whole something of a liability and is linked throughout the film with the small dog which has a terrible history of bringing bad luck. After his disillusionment with Velma, Roy slips the ring intended for her on Marie's finger. 'You don't love her any more, do you?' Marie has just asked. 'If you didn't know the answer, you wouldn't ask me.' Throughout the relationship, she is hanging on to him with varying degrees of desperation, while he comes to accept her, perhaps as the best he can hope for.

The aspect of *High Sierra* which anticipates movies from the later 'forties rather than harking back to the 'thirties is the handling of the central character. Roy Earle is neither explained, like Eddie in *The Roaring Twenties*, nor thoroughly evil like George. To contrast with him, there is a wholly dislikeable character in Krammer. But no amount of contrast can turn Roy into a nice guy like Eddie who just happens to have got into crime. Roy's *métier* is armed robbery, and he does not appear to have any scruples about it – he will unhesitatingly deal out whatever violence he feels is needed. Yet he is deeply touched by the pretty but crippled Velma and, to the extent that his predicament allows it, shows a degree of humanity, so that we are distinctly saddened when he is shot down.

There are faint suggestions of exonerating circumstances of rural poverty in his past (these might, at the time, have been assumed because such things had been laid out in the late 'thirties social movies). Roy is not a run of the mill underworld gorilla – we can sense in him potentialities that have had little chance for expression. It is allowable to interpret this waste as a comment on the society which has failed to give Roy some positive outlet. This is not spelled out as it is in *The Roaring Twenties* and *You Only Live Once* (in which fate plays as large a part as society). We are left with the feeling that there is also something within Roy that makes him criminal. The external, social reasons are not in themselves sufficient explanation.

Such explanations, in any case, only tended to cover the more wholesome lawbreakers. They never completely supplanted the assumption that there are intrinsically evil people – Bogart as Bugs Fenner and George Hally, Barton MacLane in *'G' Men* – who do not need explaining, perhaps cannot be explained. The area of operations for many 'forties and 'fifties movies was in the hinterland of uncertainty between the evil George and the explicable Eddie. Our identification is invited with a series of desperate, violent characters – later

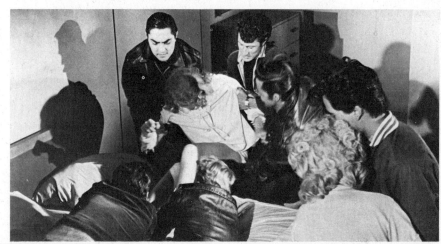

Janet Leigh in the power of the younger members of the Grande set-up in *Touch of Evil*.
Bottom:
Dennis Hopper and Sal Mineo in *Rebel Without a Cause*.

113

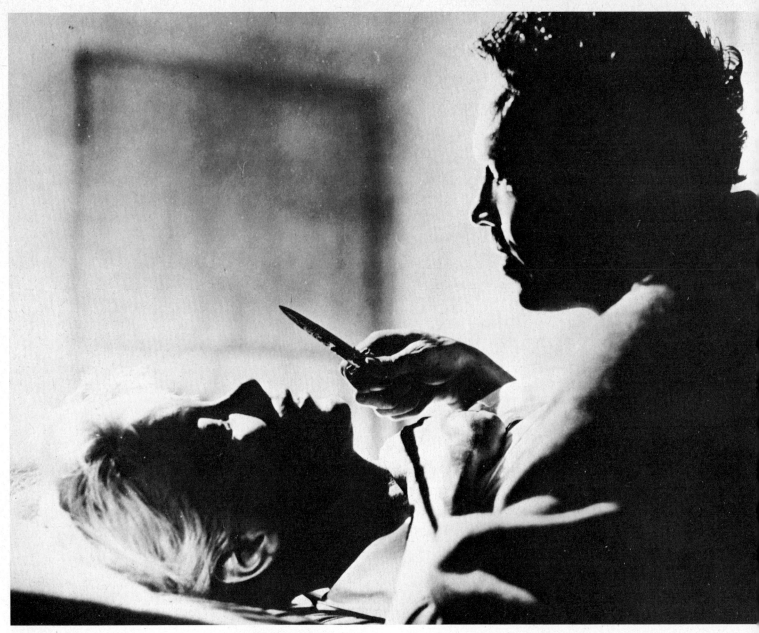

Juvenile delinquent as sexual menace – except that Warren Oates in Leslie Stevens's *Private Property* (1960) is impotent and is inclined to use a knife on Kate Manx instead.

ones included Alan Ladd as the professional killer in *This Gun for Hire* and Sterling Hayden as gangland muscle in *The Asphalt Jungle*. Our identification turns them from monsters into people because of the possibility of empathy with them. It would be exaggeration to say that identification confronts us with the potential criminal in ourselves, but at least we are made uncomfortably aware of the humanity of the wrongdoers. Our response to the crime movies of the 'forties is likely to be more complex, or at least more ambiguous, than to those of the 'thirties.

The focus from *High Sierra* onwards was often on the psyche of the gangster. The protagonist was more likely to be a tortured loner than an exemplar of society's maladjustment. An elaborately depicted milieu, often – unlike most pre-war movies – making much use of real settings, was likely, as in *The Naked City* (which was produced by Mark Hellinger) and in Robert Siodmak's *Criss Cross* (1949), to be used to situate the action rather than explain it.

The attitudes of the late 'thirties movies are answered by Robert Siodmak's *Cry of the City*

(1948) which stressed individual choice as being more crucial than social background – its two main characters are a gangster (Richard Conte) and a painstakingly honest cop (Victor Mature) who were kids together and still operate in the same neighbourhood. On the other hand, the criminal as victim theme of *You Only Live Once* reappears in the opening of Henry Hathaway's *Kiss of Death* (1947) and in Nicholas Ray's *They Live By Night* (1948); a related feeling informs the fall-guy cycle, which in films like Jacques Tourneur's *Out of the Past* (1947) reaches a level of pessimism that places them with such 'thirties French films as Marcel Carné's *Le Jour se lève* (1939). Indeed, Carné's film was remade in post-war America by Anatole Litvak as *The Long Night* (1947) with Henry Fonda instead of Jean Gabin as the doomed hero and Vincent Price taking the place of Jules Berry as the vile seducer he kills. The more sympathetic of post-war gangster heroes range from Farley Granger in *They Live By Night* through the fall guys, of whom a typical example is Burt Lancaster as the ex-con trying to go straight in *Criss Cross*, to the tragic heroes of such later pictures as Stanley Kubrick's *The Killing* (1956) and Paul Wendkos's *The Burglar* (1957). In both of these, the heroes (respectively Sterling Hayden and Dan Duryea) are established as figures of some stature, both for their evident ability and for the integrity with which they conduct their admittedly unlawful activities.

An almost inevitable consequence of concentration on gangsters as individuals was that it gave scope for the application of ideas from psychoanalysis, which had already had an impact on other art forms such as painting and literature but had penetrated the cinema only peripherally in *avant-garde* and European films such as G. W. Pabst's *Secrets of a Soul* (1926). In the popular cinema, starting with gangster movies, the impact of psychoanalysis was on the characterisation, with Henry Hathaway's *Kiss of Death* (1947) as the most spectacular early example. Richard Widmark's performance as the giggling psychopathic killer (his film début) now looks hopelessly dated, but established an alternative to social reasons and pure evil (particularly the latter) as a source of criminality. Heavies, even small-time and relatively ephemeral ones, were likely to be established as psychopathic or to show signs of some more specific deviation such as sadism. Two of Ted de Corsia's small team of hit men in *The Enforcer* (1951) display extreme psychological disturbance – we learn that Philadelphia (Jack Lambert) has been caught breaking all the windows of a railroad car and has been shipped back to the insane asylum, from which he has only been free for two weeks. The Assistant DA (Humphrey Bogart) finds him in a straitjacket. Characters were liable to be tricked out with revealing quirks of behaviour or with disabilities which might be psychosomatic in origin. Widmark as the leading hood in William Keighley's *Street with No Name* (1948) pioneered catarrh as a characteristic ailment of heavies – the inhaler has since become a reliable prop in crime movies; a much more recent example was Ross Martin's asthmatic heavy wheezing down the telephone in *An Experiment in Terror* (1962).

Right at the end of the 'forties came another crime movie directed by Raoul Walsh, *White Heat* (1949), which like its predecessor of ten years before is to some extent a summation of the crime movies of its decade. Unlike *The Roaring Twenties*, though, *White Heat* is not retrospective in treatment; rather, it unites a number of the main tendencies in 'forties gangster films. It is representative of the post-war logistic detail with which robberies were shown – it has two, beginning with a train robbery and ending with the raid on the chemical plant which the gang get into by hiding inside a specially prepared tanker truck. The framework of the film, though, is in the line of the various cinematic tributes to US Government agencies, particularly those dealing in law enforcement – this side is apparently less important in the film than it was in the original story. The main character is not an agent but a

criminal, Cody Jarrett (James Cagney).

This is a very different Cagney to his cocky, aggressive gangsters from *The Public Enemy* and *The Roaring Twenties*. He is much more an intensification of the troubled side of Roy Earle from *High Sierra*. His psychological disturbance is given a physical correlative in the head pains and the apparently epileptic fits to which he is prone. After the first attack which we witness in the film (the second he's had in a month), he says 'It's like having a red hot buzz saw inside my head.' His father died in an institution – 'He's nuts just like his old man,' says his henchman Big Ed (Steve Cochran). His brother is in an asylum – all he ever had was his mother, for whom he is

Brian Keith, Kim Novak and Guy Madison as students in *Five Against the House.*

described as having 'a fair psychopathic attachment'. Perhaps it was to increase her sympathy that he feigned headaches when he was a child; as he grew up, they became real. The attacks have the effect of reducing him to the helplessness of a small child: we see him sitting on his mother's knee. Her attitude to him is indomitably protective; she wants him to present a strong face to the rest of the gang – after the first fit, she stops him going straight back to face them: 'Not yet, don't let them see you like this – might give some of them ideas.'

Abnormal though it may be, Cody and his mother have just about the only stable and trusting relationship in the whole movie – the gang is the very antithesis of rose-tinted notions about honour among thieves. Cody believes, with some justification, that the second male member of the gang, Big Ed Somers, would be happy to put a hole in his back if it was turned for long enough. Big Ed is also having it off with Cody's sluttish wife Verna (Virginia Mayo). The other person whom Cody grows to trust is Vic Pardo (Edmond O'Brien), but Pardo is really Hank Fallon, Secret Service

John Cassavetes, Mark Rydell and Sal Mineo in *Crime in the Street*.

undercover agent, who has established himself as a friend with the single purpose of betraying him.

Where the *leitmotiv* running through *High Sierra* is the poignant reference to unattainable freedom, *White Heat* is constructed around a grim series of betrayals, culminating in the death of Cody after Fallon has alerted the police to the chemical plant robbery in which the tanker full of men is likened by Cody to the Trojan Horse and Fallon is trying to avoid being spotted by a new member of the gang who knows what he really is. When Cody is in jail, which is where Fallon is introduced into his life, Ed tries to have him killed. Verna shoots her mother-in-law in the back because she has Ed covered. After Cody has got out of prison, Ed keeps Verna in line by threatening to tell him what she did to his mother, but she gets her word in first and pins the responsibility on Ed, which means curtains for him.

Verna differs from the women in the earlier Walsh gangster films in being totally unsympathetic: she looks as if she might have a much more tarnished past than either Panama or Marie, and her current behaviour makes Velma's natural if (to Roy) disappointing desire for a good time look positively angelic. Her last act in the film is to try a deal with the cops to deliver Cody to them; the offer is rejected. Ma Jarrett (Margaret Wycherly) links back to the earlier pictures only through the maternal aspects of Panama, though she is devoid of any trace of Panama's easygoing warmth. She is the driving force behind Cody to an extent that raises questions about the reasons for the insanity of her husband and her other son; her fiercely protective attitude is akin to that of the proud mother of a gifted child. Her character can be seen in another way, too: she relates to the pioneer image of the American mother as a tower of strength – the sort of part that the same actress had played as the mother of an American hero in Howard Hawks's *Sergeant York* (1941). In *White Heat*, it is Ma who suggests when the gang leaves its hide-out after the train robbery that the casualty who is being left behind – his face has been scalded by a discharge of steam from the locomotive – might talk and should be silenced. It is Ma who makes sure that Cody gets a full share of the $57,000 haul from a job which his boys have pulled while he is in jail. And it is Ma who aims to take care of Big Ed after his treachery has been revealed. At the news of her death, Cody goes completely berserk in the prison dining-hall and ends in a straitjacket.

Cody's death is among the most extravagant in gangster movies: in the final shoot-out with the police he is at the top of a storage tank containing something dangerously flammable. Wounded but laughing, he shoots at the stopcocks on the tank and perishes in a conflagration. His epitaph, spoken by Fallon, seems an almost pointless piece of editorialising: 'He finally got to the top of the world and it blew right up in his face.'

It would be equally superfluous to say that

Richard Hartunian and Brett Halsey in *Hot Rod Rumble*.

116

Mamie Van Doren, Jean Carmen, Lori Nelson and John Russell in *Untamed Youth*.

with *White Heat* the gangster film *per se* finally burned itself out. In that particular form, Walsh's film was a rather isolated late arrival; it equally belonged with the undercover-agent cycle which was current in the late 'forties. However, it does mark at least the temporary end of the series of gangster movies, mainly from Warner Brothers, which had been in progress since the early 'thirties; in the years after it appeared, there were no notable films which seem to belong within what might be called the Warner gangster-story tradition. When gangster stories re-emerged in quantity in the late 'fifties, the framework had changed to the partly fictional biographies of the nostalgia cycle. Among the successors to *White Heat*, John Huston's *The Asphalt Jungle* is more in the mould of gangster tragedy, a species that has turned up from time to time, notably in *The Killing*. Huston showed a changed situation in which, as Richard Whitehall points out, 'a loyalty and camaraderie within the social unit of the gang is displaced by a hire and fire business basis'. (The change is neither sudden nor total: the gang in *White Heat* was hardly held together by camaraderie, and self-contained gangs exist later in, for example, *Violent Saturday*.) The 'fifties were a period of diversification in crime movies, with new emphases, new crimes, and new heavies.

The year 1950 saw the start of Kefauver Committee hearings which provided a mass of documentation that shaped the assumption of crime movies thereafter. The Committee's revelations may not have done much for the law-enforcement agencies which were hooked on winkling out commie agents, but they established large-scale criminal organisation as an element in the movies, starting rather tentatively with *The Enforcer* (1951). The Communists, however, failed to make it as cinematic heavies; in spite of the opportunities

that the anti-Communist cycle offered for conspicuous flag-waving or ritual expiation, in business terms, it was clearly a loser.

During the 'fifties, gangsters in movies were evolving towards the soberly suited uniformity of business executives, which was consonant with a view of organised crime as a parallel to big business. The perfect sartorial conformism achieved by Lee Marvin and Clu Gulager in Don Siegel's *The Killers* (1964) was an expression of corporate discipline which was the reverse of the untrammelled enterprise of the free-lance days.

The 'fifties also saw an increased insistence on crime as being part of the world in which ordinary citizens exist, not just a contest between gangsters and cops but a menace to the entire population. Police wives rubbed out by organised crime with bombs meant for their husbands and the arbitrary targets of individual

Russ Tamblyn, Jan Sterling and Mamie Van Doren in *High School Confidential*.

Latter-day motor-cycle
movie: *C.C. and Company*
(1970).

Andy Devine, Janet Leigh,
Jack Webb and Edmond
O'Brien in *Pete Kelly's Blues*.

118

deranged snipers are only two varieties of victim. In Phil Karlson's *Kansas City Confidential* (1952), John Payne was a totally innocent party with a criminal record who got the blame for a robbery executed by Preston Foster's trio of hoods (Jack Elam, Neville Brand and Lee Van Cleef – it was a vintage film for heavies) and had to spend the bulk of the movie extricating himself. There is a very different treatment of the predicament of an innocent man who is accused of a crime in Alfred Hitchcock's *The Wrong Man* (1957). In *The Enforcer*, a cab-driver and his daughter have the misfortune to enter a café at the moment that Everett Sloane is personally inaugurating his contract murder business by doing a job on the café-owner with a handy butcher knife. Later, when the business is flourishing, the driver recognises a passenger in his cab as being the killer, but when he goes for his evening shave, Ted de Corsia, the executive arm of Sloane's enterprise, is lurking there to take over on the razor work. The daughter changes her name and moves; her room-mate, wrongly fingered, is killed, and she is only just saved by Assistant DA Humphrey Bogart when Sloane realises the mistake.

In a cluster of 'fifties movies, ordinary people fall, usually by complete chance, into the power of the heavies who take possession of their homes, their children or, in Ida Lupino's *The Hitch-hiker* (1953) and Irvin Kershner's *The Young Captives* (1959), their automobiles. The families whose lives are invaded by criminals could have been selected as representative of middle America, as law-abiding a collection of citizens as one can imagine – for earlier crime movies, these people would have belonged in the audience rather than on the screen. Although Alfred Hitchcock's *The Man Who Knew Too Much* (1956) is a remake of a picture which Hitchcock made in Britain in 1934, it is related to this group of films – the couple's son (daughter in the first version) is kidnapped to prevent the father from divulging what he might have learned accidentally about an assassination attempt. There the family is American but the setting is exotic; Lewis Allen's *Suddenly* (1954), William Wyler's *The Desperate Hours* (1955)

Lee Marvin in *Violent Saturday*.

Baby Face Nelson. Mickey Rooney and Carolyn Jones as Mr and Mrs Lester Gillis. *Above:* with shady doctor (Sir Cedric Hardwicke).

Right: Nelson mortally wounded.

120

and two films by Andrew Stone, *The Night Holds Terror* (1955) and *Cry Terror* (1958), all involve families in their own homes confronted out of the blue with a situation of extreme menace.

Suddenly, which turns out to be the name of a place in California, is, like Hitchcock's film, about political assassination, but here the target is the President of the United States whose train is scheduled to stop at the town. A hired killer (Frank Sinatra) sets himself up with a rifle in a house that is a good vantage point. As in all these pictures, the family fights back and eliminates him – here by the expedient of wiring his gun up to a high-tension point on their television set.

The Desperate Hours, like other latter-day William Wyler movies, laboriously spells out what other less prestige-laden efforts would handle very much better by implication. A trio of escaping convicts (Humphrey Bogart, his brother Dewey Martin and the simple but brutal Robert Middleton) select a house in the residential neighbourhood of a mid-western town as a place to lay low and make contact with the girl who is bringing their money to them. The house is occupied by business executive Fredric March, his wife Martha Scott, their grown-up daughter Mary Murphy and young son Richard Eyer. The tensions between the two sides are carefully laid out for us. 'Your dad knows what side it's buttered,' says Bogart to the boy – he takes exception to March's careful, calculating mind and makes snide remarks about his position and intelligence, particularly after he has discovered that March has only $800 in the bank. Later, Bogart's resentment becomes more specific: he says that there were men like March on the parole board. His hate of comfortable bourgeois society (and March may have little cash in the bank but he can generate sufficient cash flow to maintain a very satisfactory standard of living) is at variance with the envy felt by his younger brother for such snug normality – he tells Bogart: 'You taught me everything except how to live in a house like this.'

What was intended as an overnight stay is extended because the woman bringing the money runs a red light in Columbus, Ohio, and is pursued by the local traffic cops in spite of the fact that she is being tailed by the FBI; she escapes and ditches the car. Instead of bringing the money, she is told by Bogart to mail it to Frederic March's office. As a result March and his daughter have to pursue their daily routine of office work to avoid attracting attention – the process is complicated by the girl having a persistent suitor (Gig Young). The man who comes round to collect the garbage is taken for a ride in his own truck by Robert Middleton because he may have got suspicious at the sight of an unfamiliar car in the garage.

Even before the convicts' stay has been extended, there is an attempt to fight back. The daughter pretends to faint and then bites Dewey Martin; her parents join in overpowering him and getting his gun – at this point, Bogart is out in the garage disciplining Robert

Charles Bronson in the title-part of Roger Corman's *Machine Gun Kelly* (1958).

Middleton with a touch of pistol-whipping. The flaw in the otherwise well-improvised counter-attack is that the son who has been told to shut himself in his bedroom has been equally enterprising and has shinned down a handy tree on the way to raise the alarm and has fallen straight into the hands of Bogart.

The family's failure is symptomatic of the effects of the gang on them: confronted with such a threat, March has quite a bit of difficulty keeping his own family in line. With the family so evidently standing for the quintessence of American society (a frightening thought as its members are so uniformly boring), we are being sold the thought that crime is striking at the very roots of all that is sacred in American life. When March voices his reactions, the enormity of his outrage is concomitant with a threat of this dimension; he also demonstrates how the poison of violence can infect the very fabric of America. He tells Bogart: 'I understand how your mind works because I've got the same thing in me – I want to kill you and if anything goes wrong, so help me God, I will.' And in case we have not got the point, the climax of the film has March pointing a gun (provided by the law which now has the house surrounded) at Bogart who says, 'You ain't got it in you.' So March comes across with the punch-line: 'I got it in me – you put it there.' But having said that, and because he is meant to be a nice guy, March does not deliver (he has accepted a gun but no bullets). Instead of underlining his aphorism with lead, March tells Bogart about the demise of Dewey Martin before ordering him out of the house, a piece of social isolationism that would be hard to believe even if we had been offered evidence of anything that was really worth protecting within the March family's defensible space. Bogart goes out and gets himself gunned down by the waiting police.

Another way of bringing crime closer to the man in the street was to deal with crimes committed by people who did not belong to the

121

criminal classes. There was a brief flowering of such movies in the mid 'forties: Billy Wilder's *Double Indemnity* (1944), Fritz Lang's *The Woman in the Window* (1944, in which the whole sordid business was in a dream by the apparent killer, Edward G. Robinson), Lang's *Scarlet Street* (1945), Michael Curtiz's *Mildred Pierce* (1945, with Joan Crawford's daughter, Ann Blyth, turning out to be the killer) and Tay Garnett's *The Postman Always Rings Twice* (1946). In Anatole Litvak's *Sorry, Wrong Number* (1948), an invalid but rich Barbara Stanwyck realises that her husband, Burt Lancaster, is trying to kill her (a contemporary echo of a celebrated period movie, Robert Siodmak's *The Spiral Staircase* (1946), in which a dumb Dorothy McGuire is the potential murder victim). Many of these films are hybrids between the crime movie and the woman's picture, a combination most notably exemplified by another Robert Siodmak movie, *The File on Thelma Jordan* (1949), in which a married and hitherto upright Assistant DA (Wendell Corey) is seduced by a former gambling hostess (Barbara Stanwyck). When her rich maiden aunt is murdered and she is arrested, she persuades him to take the prosecution case and blow it. He does better than that by also anonymously hiring the defence attorney. After she has been found not guilty, the denouement includes self-sacrifice (a car crash which kills her evil lover) and a deathbed confession of love; Corey, it emerges, has already come clean to the DA.

The few 'fifties films that have crimes committed by apparently ordinary people include some more modest efforts: Andrew Stone's *The Steel Trap* (1952) in which Joseph Cotten steals money from the bank which he manages and another Andrew Stone movie, *Blueprint for Murder* (1953) which has a heroine (Jean Peters) who turns out to be a cold-blooded poisoner. In a 3-D movie, Roy Baker's *Inferno* (1953), millionaire Robert Ryan is left to die in

Rod Steiger as *Al Capone*. *Opposite: The Grissom Gang* — members jubilant at collecting $1,000,000 ransom for Miss Blandish; Irene Dailey, Don Keefer, Ralph Waite, Tony Musante and Joey Faye.

Rod Steiger and Joe De Santis in *Al Capone*.

123

Above and right: The Rise and Fall of Legs Diamond with Ray Danton (above).

Ray Danton as Legs Diamond and Robert Lowery as Arnold Rothstein, with Judson Pratt and Elaine Stewart in *The Rise and Fall of Legs Diamond*.

the desert by his wife Rhonda Fleming and her lover William Lundigan after he has been thrown from his horse and broken a leg. A much more alarming picture in its implication of abnormality as a norm is Howard W. Koch's *The Girl in Black Stockings* (1957). This starts with a stock romantic image: a couple (Lex Barker and Anne Bancroft) dancing to soft music at night beside a pool. The idyll comes to a sudden halt when she lights a cigarette: she sees something illuminated by the lighter flame and screams. The something is a mutilated corpse. There are plenty of suspects around, for example an embittered Ron Randell who is paralysed in all four limbs and is looked after by a very fierce sister (Marie Windsor). The paralysis is psychosomatic and happened after a girl walked out on him. After a few more deaths, Barker realises that the murderer is Anne Bancroft, who has been apparently one of the more normal people around. In fact, she has a history of murder going back ten years to when she lost the man she loved to her sister. The nice girl of the opening sequence and

indeed most of the picture has escaped from an institution.

During the 'fifties, Hollywood, scared by the depredations of television, tried harder than ever before to relate to its audience – it is possible that it was actually trying in earnest for the first time, as previously it apparently had only to manufacture a relatively glamorous product for people to appear obediently at the box office in ever-increasing numbers. The film industry, which had been used to operating in well-heeled isolation, was not ideally equipped to identify new forms with which it could attract the public. The 'fifties was a period of casting around for suitable new ideas which were then likely to be forced by producers into the traditional moulds which they could understand. In a decade which produced a range of enterprises from technical ventures like Cinerama and Vistavision to largely abortive attempts at plundering talent from television (in a group of films that included *Marty* and *Twelve Angry Men*), the new subject areas included youth and drugs.

Of these related subjects, the drug cycle was much the less important. It dealt with the woes of the consumer and used the pusher as a lurid heavy – Darren McGavin as Louie in the first of the series, Otto Preminger's *The Man with the Golden Arm* (1955), and Henry Silva as Mother in Fred Zinnemann's *A Hatful of Rain* (1957). The heroes were decent chaps struggling under the burden of addiction like Cameron Mitchell in Andre De Toth's *Monkey on my Back* (1957). Other entries in the drug cycle were strictly B-features like Joseph M. Newman's *Death in Small Doses* (1957), which looked at the supply of benzedrine tablets to long-distance truck-drivers and was basically a crime movie rather than a study of addiction (a form so inherently unenjoyable for the audience that it quickly disappeared and has hardly been seen again except for Jerry Schatzberg's *Panic in Needle Park* in 1971). From Don Siegel's *The Line Up* (1958), drugs became a commodity as important to illegal trafficking in crime pictures as liquor had been in the 'thirties gangster movies, providing the mainspring of the action in such pictures as William Friedkin's *The French Connection* (1971), and Gordon Parks's *The Super Cops* (1974). The drug movies did not throw up any equivalent of the extrovert racketeer protagonist of the 'thirties pictures: the central characters of *The Line Up* belong among the contract killers of the organised-crime movies. It was only in the rather specialised context of the black movie that the dealer made his appearance in the main role with Ron O'Neal in Gordon Parks Jr's *Superfly* (1972).

Hollywood's attempts at youth appeal were the result of a realisation that the kids were becoming the mainstay of movie audiences while their parents stayed at home loving Lucy. Simple commercial logic indicated the wisdom of appealing to the young, a conclusion which was conspicuously at variance with the inclination of many of the guys who had to deliver

Neville Brand as Al Capone in *The Scarface Mob*.

starring James Dean, and Richard Brooks's *The Blackboard Jungle*. The Dean films both centred on the alienation of the young from their parents and the values which they represented; Brooks's film, based on an Evan Hunter novel, was about a New York public school teacher (Glenn Ford) faced with hostility and violence in his classroom. This trio of very honourable movies, one of which was even a period picture, opened up a new idea for Hollywood: juvenile delinquency. Its treatment quickly degenerated to pictures, in Richard Brooks's words, 'about kids running around hitting each other with chains': the same year as *Rebel Without a Cause* saw an early effort in the juvenile-delinquency cheapie field, *Teenage Crime Wave*. One of the more peculiar earlier entrants in the youth market was Phil Karlson's *Five Against the House* (1955) in which a group of elderly college students including Kevin McCarthy, Brian Keith, Alvy Moore and Kim Novak decide to rob a casino for the fun of showing that it can be done. Brian Keith, however, once suffered a head injury and is prone to fits of uncontrollable rage. . . .

From 1956, teenage appeal was to be seen in a variety of guises from the rock 'n' roll pictures which started with *Rock Around the Clock* (1956) to that peculiar mutation, the teenage horror picture, such as *I Was a Teenage Werewolf* (1957). The majority of the youth cycle, though, seized upon the exploitable elements of juvenile delinquency which could be identified in the more respectable pioneers of the cycle: the black-leather jackets of the motor-cycle gangs, the teenage knife fights, the chicken runs and the attitudes ranging from rebellion against authority to self-destructive wildness. The mid 'fifties produced a few more films that offered some considered treatment of youth problems: Don Siegel's *Crime in the Streets* (1956), with a rather laborious script from a television play by Reginald Rose, deals with teenage violence in a poor urban neighbourhood, while John Frankenheimer's first film, *The Young Stranger* (1957), is a quiet, minor-key successor to *Rebel Without a Cause*, showing the bewilderment of prosperous parents – father is a movie executive – when their son (James MacArthur) briefly abandons bourgeois restraint and gets himself arrested after hitting a rather offensive cinema-manager.

These pictures were very much the exception: 1957 was the year that the teenage exploitation movie really got under way. The nature of the products and even their tawdry, low-budget appearance is nicely summed up by a selection of the year's titles: *Dragstrip Girl, Reform School Girl, Motor Cycle Gang, Teenage Doll, Hot Rod Rumble, Untamed Youth*. This last is mildly diverting, being in the circumstances competently made by Howard W. Koch and having as a young convict the singer Eddie Cochran. Its main characters, though, are two 'entertainers', Mamie Van Doren and Lori Nelson, who are convicted of vagrancy, which appears to mean bathing naked in a pool by the roadside. They get sent to do some forced

the goods. The sanitised vision of teenage life disseminated by many a major studio movie (with Fox as the worst offender) seemed designed less to please the kids than to avoid offending the blue-rinse audience. No real environment could ever have been wholesome enough to accommodate the open-faced, blonde pony-tailed girls who virginally inhabited Hollywood's teenage wonderland, which developed in the Gidget series and finally petered out in the beach-party movies of the early 'sixties.

The youth picture began in earnest in 1955, although it had been anticipated in the previous year by a first essay in one of its main varieties, the motor-cycle-gang movie, Laslo Benedek's *The Wild One*, starring such mature motor-cyclists as Marlon Brando and Lee Marvin. In 1955 came Elia Kazan's *East of Eden* and Nicholas Ray's *Rebel Without a Cause*, both

Pretty Boy Floyd with John Ericson.

labour on a farm whose owner has an arrangement with the local lady judge (and is secretly married to her). The main originators of these teenage exploitation movies were American International, an outfit with none of the inhibitions of the major studios. They made none of the majors' attempts to reach the widest possible audience. Instead, they decided exactly who they were aiming to satisfy and tailored their product accordingly. Thus, for example, they kept parents and other figures of adult authority as far as possible out of the picture in order to avoid difficulty over the attitude the films should take to them. Also the kids preferred movies without them.

The following year brought a variant in the group of school exposé movies pioneered by the producer Albert Zugsmith whose previous work had included classier items directed by Douglas Sirk and Orson Welles. This series started with *High School Confidential* (1958) and continued with *Platinum High School* (1960) and *College Confidential* (1960). The final phase of the films about juvenile delinquency was the motor-cycle-gang movie, initiated by Roger Corman's *The Wild Angels* (1966), which was inspired by the phenomenon of the Hell's Angels, some of whose adherents from Venice, California, filled out the ranks of cyclists in the

picture. The following year produced follow-ups including *Devil's Angels, Hell on Wheels, Hell's Angels on Wheels*, with *Angels from Hell* roaring up in 1968 and *Hell's Angels* in 1969. The genre with a related group of hot-rod movies has continued in more modest quantities in the mid 'seventies, but as a staple subject juvenile delinquency and related mani-

The George Raft Story. Ray Danton as Raft tells New York gangster boss Joe De Santis that he wants to make a career in showbusiness rather than crime (with Frank Gorshin, *below*) and learns from Captain of Detectives Emile Meyer that the police department is going to be his severest critic.

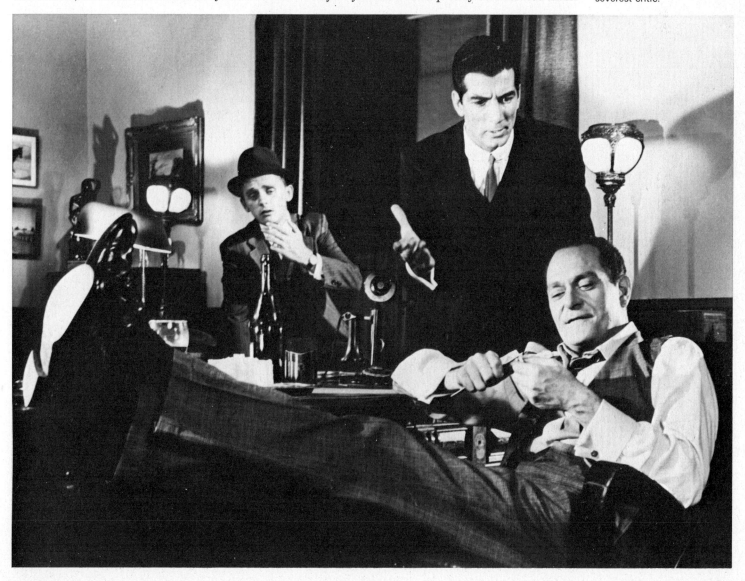

127

Getaway in *Bonnie and Clyde*: Michael J. Pollard, Gene Hackman, Warren Beatty and Faye Dunaway.

Warren Beatty as Clyde Barrow and Faye Dunaway as Bonnie Parker in *Bonnie and Clyde*.

festations had their cinematic boom in the second half of the 'fifties, since when, apart from the Hell's Angels movies, they have been in decline.

The new genres of the 'fifties, the organised-crime movies and the juvenile-delinquency movies, largely filled the gangster-movie niche during the decade. But even before the gangster protagonist made a come-back with the nostalgia cycle, there were occasional crime movies which had more in common with earlier patterns than with the current product so far as relationships within the gang were concerned.

Two of these films are very much the work of young directors trying to establish their reputations by producing formally striking movies within an established and thus saleable genre. *The Burglar* (1957) was the first feature directed by Paul Wendkos, and although Stanley Kubrick had made two features before *The Killing* (1956), these were minutely budgeted efforts made far outside the confines of the film industry (though the second of them, *Killer's Kiss*, is remarkable for Kubrick's photography of New York locations – it was bought for distribution by United Artists). *The Burglar* starts off with a Wellesian flourish of newsreels and a burglary from the house of a rich religious eccentric. Most of the film, though, is about the tensions within the gang while it is holed up waiting for the heat to die down, and particularly about the relationship between the ageing burglar (Dan Duryea) and the daughter (Jayne Mansfield) of a dead mentor. The last sequences gain their atmosphere from the desolation of a crummy

seaside resort and have the same feeling of sadness as the end of François Truffaut's *Shoot the Pianist*, a rather dottier adaptation from the same writer, David Goodis.

The Killing is a piece of logistic bravura, describing an elaborately organised race-track robbery which uses the shooting of the leading horse in a big race as a diversionary action. The story is not handled in the conventional manner of alternating between more or less simultaneous developments, but, helped by some intermittently irritating narration to tell us the time, follows one character at a time and then goes back to an earlier point to pick up the story of another character and bring that up to date. The organiser of the job is a small-time criminal (Sterling Hayden) tired of 'going for peanuts' who tries to get the one big haul that will allow him to start a new life. The other participants, though, are not all habitual criminals: the cop (Ted De Corsia) who has got into debt, the teller at a betting window at the track (Elisha Cook Jr) who has a flashy discontented wife (Marie Windsor). This lady also

Faye Dunaway and Warren Beatty pose for a photograph in *Bonnie and Clyde*.

Shelley Winters as Ma Barker and Don Stroud as her son, with his brothers in *Bloody Mama*.

Warren Oates as John
Dillinger leaves Little
Bohemia in *Dillinger*.

Warren Oates in *Dillinger*.

has a boy friend (Vince Edwards) who tries to take over the proceeds. As in *The Burglar*, the ending of the film communicates a sense of loss because of the standing that the hero has gained in our eyes – Hayden is not killed; the suitcase containing the stolen money falls off an airport baggage-truck and bursts scattering a snow of banknotes. The police arrive and Hayden, rather than shoot it out, resignedly gives himself up.

These two pictures, with their sympathetic criminals and melancholy conclusions, are iconographically isolated efforts, which are to some extent throw-backs to the world of the 'forties gangster movies. Richard Fleischer's *Violent Saturday* (1955), written by Sidney Boehm, is unusual in a different way, for the extent to which it mixes genres and brings together a variety of the strands of 'fifties Hollywood film-making. It is even typical commercially of the sort of package being offered by major studios, particularly Fox, at the time, with a heap of second-rate, played-out or aspiring stars taking the place of any really major figures. *Violent Saturday* had, among others, Richard Egan, Victor Mature, Virginia Leith, Stephen McNally and Sylvia Sidney. It is a bank hold-up picture, with McNally arriving in the small town of Bradenville to case the joint and posing as a costume-jewellery salesman. His partners in crime are Lee Marvin, who is suffering from a bad cold, and J. Carroll Naish, who is described as real mean but is a stickler for appearance: 'Nothing like looking neat and clean for a stick-up.'

But unlike most bank-robbery pictures, this one is concerned with the community that is robbed as much as it is with the robbers. It links the invaded-home movies like *The Desperate Hours* with the small-town emotional dramas like *Peyton Place*, which appeared a couple of years later. It even relates to the 'fifties series of weak town/strong man westerns. The *Peyton Place* side of the picture, the seamy side of the primmest area of American life, emerged in the bank manager watching the nurse's window as she goes to bed, the old lady involved in petty theft, and the problems of the richest couple in town – Richard Egan's wife tells him: 'We can't change – not us. You're an alcoholic and I'm a tramp.' But Egan is in love with the nurse who's being spied on by the manager whose bank is going to be robbed. Mature, the successful, happily married manager of the alcoholic's mine, occupies a similar position to Fredric March in *The Desperate Hours*. The film also contains another theme not unknown in 'fifties Hollywood, the impossibility of pacifism in the face of an unavoidable threat. This is represented by Ernest Borgnine, a member of the Amish sect. He is archaic in speech and non-violent by conviction, but ends up planting a pitchfork in the back of Lee Marvin who is about to take another shot at an already wounded Victor Mature. If some future student of American culture were to look for the movie that best summarised the work of Hollywood in the 'fifties, *Violent Saturday*, a very accomplished piece of work, could be a strong candidate for his attention.

The year of *Violent Saturday* also saw the first harbinger of the nostalgia cycle of crime movies. Jack Webb's *Pete Kelly's Blues* (1955) was about a jazz band in the 'twenties and was

131

sold more on the musicians than on the gangsters – its stars included Peggy Lee and Ella Fitzgerald. But the band played in speakeasies and came under the thumb of gangster Edmond O'Brien and so it is a crime movie as well. In many ways, though, it belongs with the opening parts of Anthony Mann's *The Glenn Miller Story* (1953) and with Charles Vidor's *Love Me or Leave Me* (1955), a Doris Day musical with gangster relationships as it is a biography of Ruth Etting. The references to real people in *Pete Kelly's Blues*, however, are to the bandleader Jean Goldkette rather than to, say, Capone.

The nostalgia cycle started in earnest with Don Siegel's *Baby Face Nelson* (1957), a biography of Lester Gillis alias George 'Baby Face' Nelson, one of the most palpably insane of 'thirties gunmen and briefly a colleague of John Dillinger. Like virtually all its successors it

refers to the historical record for reference points but otherwise sets off on its own for everything except the broadest of character sketches. In the context of this book, these films present something of a problem. Nelson and Dillinger died forty years ago, in 1934; they are nearer in time to the exploits of Butch Cassidy and the Wild Bunch, which continued until 1901, than they are to the present day. Indeed, the treatment in these films is much like that accorded to Jesse James or Doc Holliday in westerns. Yet Nelson and Dillinger were alive when the earliest films mentioned in this book were made.

Crime movies are dealt with here as works related, however tenuously, to current or recent actuality. There is a crucial difference between the retrospective picture offered by *The Roaring Twenties* and that presented in, say, *The Rise and Fall of Legs Diamond*. For most of the audience that watched Walsh's picture, Prohibition and the Depression were memories sufficiently real and recent to keep much of their pain. The historical crime movies of the past fifteen years are aimed at an audience which would not remember these things. Many members of the audience for John Milius's *Dillinger* (1973) would have parents born after the death of the film's subject. These films, then, are more akin to westerns in their use of an approximately historical context than they are either to the crime films from the period they cover or to current crime movies. Just as the films have it both ways, as history and as fiction, I feel entitled to utilise the visuals as very approximate history and largely to pass over the films because they do not belong with other crime pictures.

A few of the nostalgia cycle are entirely fictional: the most notable are Nicholas Ray's *Party Girl* (1958), which nevertheless has a leading heavy with strong Capone references, and Robert Aldrich's *The Grissom Gang* (1971) which takes James Hadley Chase's novel 'No Orchids for Miss Blandish' (previously and, at the time, notoriously filmed in Britain in 1948) and equips it with some of the mystique of the

Paul Winfield in *Gordon's War*.

Ron O'Neal in *Superfly*.

Barker gang and the Freudian sexual dimension that had been introduced to the genre by Arthur Penn's *Bonnie and Clyde* (1967). The nearest thing to an accurate biography was probably Richard Wilson's *Al Capone* (1959), though Capone's most famous operation was shown in laborious detail in Roger Corman's uninteresting and often poorly acted staging of *The St Valentine's Day Massacre* (1967) which uses a commentary to hold the threads of the action together in a manner that echoes Stanley Kubrick's *The Killing*. Usually, the historical pretensions are very slight. Jim Kitses mentions that for *The Rise and Fall of Legs Diamond* (1960), the director, Budd Boetticher, was given considerable freedom so long as the film kept its distance from the facts. The same year gave us John Ericson as *Pretty Boy Floyd* and pictures about *Murder Incorporated* and about *The Purple Gang* which had operated in Detroit during the 'twenties. In 1961, Vic Morrow was Arthur Flegenheimer alias Dutch Schultz in *Portrait of a Mobster*, with Ray Danton doing a guest spot as Legs Diamond, John Davis Chandler impersonated *Mad Dog Coll* and David Jansen played the name-part in Joseph M. Newman's *The Story of Arnold Rothstein*. Newman also produced a variant on the genre in *The George Raft Story* (1961), with Ray Danton as Raft and Neville Brand doing his *Untouchables* number as Al Capone.

After a few years largely in abeyance, the historical cycle was revived by the appearance of its most strikingly original (and financially most successful) picture, Arthur Penn's *Bonnie and Clyde* (1967), which does not content itself with biography but is historical in a similar way to Elia Kazan's *Wild River* or Luchino Visconti's *The Leopard*, integrating its story with a portrait of a society at a particular moment in time – a much more ambitious undertaking than the mere conveying of 'period feeling', the stock-in-trade of even the crummiest of the genre. Roger Corman's *Bloody Mama* (1970) was yet another treatment of an old favourite, Ma Barker, this time with a heavy emphasis on the incest angle.

Another collection of nostalgic items appears to be on the way: a biography of Louis 'Lepke' Buchalter has already been made (with Tony Curtis in the lead) and one on Bugsy Siegel is coming. The first of the new bunch was John Milius's *Dillinger* (1973), which is clearly more interested in the character of the G-man, Melvin Purvis (Ben Johnson), than in Dillinger himself, though he is admirably played by Warren Oates. Purvis, who appears from his photographs to have been a rather unprepossessing individual, is built up to represent the whole inexorable weight of the FBI. Before each elimination of a public enemy, he lights a cigar from a box given to him by one of his agents the day before he was killed. Dillinger is also portrayed as recognising that his contest with the FBI operates through the media as well as on the ground and therefore pays attention to his public image. 'These few dollars you've lost here today,' he tells the victims of a bank robbery, 'could have bought you stories to tell your children. . . . This could be one of the great moments in your life. Don't make it your last.' The film makes a great show of being a document of the period: Farm Security Administration photographs are used under the credits and titles are used initially to name the main FBI agents and then to specify the locations and year of each important scene. Yet it takes enormous liberties with the historical facts, for example in placing Baby Face Nelson's death before Dillinger's rather than four months later. The film is not so much about facts as about legends. It is particularly engaging in its view of Nelson (Richard Dreyfuss) who tells Dillinger: 'I got my own way of taking banks. I go in shooting, I kill everybody in sight and I take the money. Very easy, it works very well. You don't like it, you get somebody else.'

Finally, in this chapter, a brief mention of the black movie, which has latched on to the crime movie as it has to every other genre, though perhaps with more conviction here than elsewhere. We have had black cops in *Cotton Comes to Harlem* and its sequel *Come Back Charleston Blue*, black private eyes (*Shaft* and *Black Eye*), black secret agents (*Cleopatra Jones*), black vigilante squads (*Gordon's War* and *Foxy Brown*) and black muscling-in on the Mafia (*Black Caesar*, known in Britain as *The Godfather of Harlem*). The black crime movie has also furnished a concept of its very own, particularly in Gordon Parks Jr's *Superfly* (1972): the cocaine-pusher is the hero, implicitly because his success is in itself an assault on the white business/crime/police continuum. The idea that black criminals are only the puppets of evil white men who operate in curtain-walled isolation from the ghetto is to be found in other black movies including *Gordon's War* and *Hammer*. But *Superfly* goes further than any of the others by making Priest (Ron O'Neal) the loner scoring points at the expense of the white establishment, which has the city's Deputy Commissioner of Police as the main supplier of cocaine. We are confronted with the curious spectacle of Warner Brothers here and American International in other black exploitation movies backing and thereby profiting from pictures attacking the white capitalist power structure which must include themselves.

THE ORGANISATION

'"'There's this ridiculous scene in the end where two brothers kiss, and then one brother takes a gun and shoots the other," Bill said. "It's real Hollywood crap."' The film is Martin Ritt's *The Brotherhood* (1968) and the critic is Bill Bonanno, recorded in Gay Talese's family chronicle 'Honor Thy Father', giving the opinion that this first big-budget American Mafia movie was one of the most stupid films ever made. He was not simply expressing the snobbish view of the Hollywood product that he might have picked up along with his university education. He had, after all, a degree of authority as eldest son and heir of Joseph Bonanno, popularly known as Joe Bananas, the don of one of New York's five Mafia families.

The subject of the film had been raised over family lunch by Bill Bonanno's mother-in-law, the widow of another don, Joseph Profaci; seeing the picture at Radio City, she had been moved to tears by a scene which reminded her of her husband. At this point in March 1969, Bonanno was part of the way through reading a newly published novel, Mario Puzo's 'The Godfather', and admired the author's 'insight into the secret society. Bill found the central figure in the novel, Don Vito Corleone, a believable character, and he wondered if the name had been partly inspired by "Don Vito" Genovese and by the town of Corleone, which was in the interior of western Sicily south-east of Castellamare. Bill believed that his own father possessed many of the quietly sophisticated qualities that the writer attributed to Don Vito Corleone, and yet there were also elements in the character that reminded Bill of the late Thomas Lucchese.'

The Mafia as a theme for narrative entertain-

Previous page: Tolly Devlin sees four shadows on a wall kill his father in Samuel Fuller's *Underworld USA*. *Right:* Lee Marvin in *Point Blank*.

Alex Cord embraces Kirk
Douglas before shooting him
at the end of *The
Brotherhood*.

Joseph Bologna as Bill
Bonanno and his father
(Raf Vallone) in *Honor Thy
Father*.

ments really arrived in the last two years of the 'sixties – Peter Maas's book, 'The Valachi Papers', was published in 1968. This may seem a long time after 1963 and Joseph Valachi's televised revelations which were in turn prompted to some extent by the memoirs of a more senior Mafia figure, Nicola Gentile, obtained a few years before by the Special Group of the Department of Justice, which had been disbanded before the document could be published. However, Valachi's appearances before the McClellan Committee had been something of a disaster, and Maas was not authorised to do the Valachi book until late 1965. Even after Maas's and Puzo's books had established the Mafia as a subject in its own right rather than an amorphous enemy of the law, its arrival in the cinema was not helped by the egg laid at the box office by *The Brotherhood*. This flop – the only real precedent available – was enough to give Paramount serious misgivings about the financial viability of *The Godfather* as a movie.

The public interest in the Mafia has encouraged the idea that the Mafia is synonymous with organised crime. In an industry employing over 100,000 full-time gangsters, a probable number of 5,000 mafiosi are less of a force in the economics of crime than they have been made to seem by the exposure of their secret society's intricate conventions. The power of the Mafia in America, increased enormously in the 'twenties by Prohibition, preceded its organisation above family level. The climax of the Mafia's internal feuding was the Castellammarese War of 1930 which, like the preceding skirmishes, had its roots in the transference of social structures from the more primitive areas of Italy where most of the powerful men in the Mafia had been born. The most powerful of all was Joe 'The Boss' Masseria whose main obstacle to supremacy was a particularly large and tightly knit group from Castellammare del Golfo in Sicily under the leadership of Salvatore Maranzano. The slaughter of the war between Masseria's forces and Maranzano's ended when Lucky Luciano and Vito Genovese secretly changed sides and Masseria got shot

in the back after a convivial lunch with Luciano. Maranzano, now *capo di tutti capi*, called a meeting to set out a new structure which would cut out the feuding. Less than five months later, in September 1931, Maranzano was rubbed out in his office by hired Jewish killers from the Bug and Meyer Mob. In the wake of this killing and under the direction of Luciano, about forty other old-fashioned Italian-born mafiosi, the Greasers or Mustache Petes, were eliminated and the Mafia was thereafter run by a commission of nine, made up from bosses of the twenty-four families in the United States, serving in rotation. Thanks to this set-up, the internal strife which had attracted unwelcome attention to the Mafia was kept under control until the Banana War of the 'sixties.

Much more important developments, though, had started with the first national convention of gang leaders back in May 1929 at the Hotel President in Atlantic City. This meeting, which brought together the Italian and Jewish elements of crime, was founded on a crucial meeting of minds between Al Capone's mentor, Johnny Torrio, and Meyer Lansky, the brain of the Bug and Meyer Mob. Its outcome was a cartel fixing the illegal liquor trade, the so-called Big Seven, which included such non-Latin figures as Harry Stromberg, otherwise known as Nig Rosen, from Cleveland and Abner 'Longie' Zwillman from New Jersey. The ethnic mixture was a trailer for the ultimate recipe of organised crime, the Syndicate, which was set up in its definitive form at a get-together in spring 1934 at a New York hotel, allegedly the Waldorf Astoria (a hostelry which Luciano favoured with his patronage for some years, maintaining a suite there under the name of Charles Ross). In the years since the first meeting, the groundwork had been laid by a co-operative venture in the Molaska Corporation, which was set up in November 1933 to manufacture illicit and thus untaxed liquor. The Mafia was now in a form which could be integrated into a National Crime Syndicate because of its acquisition of organisation and the

Gangster imagery in a 'fifties comedy, Frank Tashlin's *The Girl Can't Help It* (1956). *Below:* Edmond O'Brien as Marty 'Fats' Murdock and Henry Jones as his sidekick Mousey convincing a bar-owner that he would like to install one of their juke-boxes. *Left:* a newsreel from the days when he was Marty 'Slim' Murdock.

141

The Saint Valentine's Day Massacre and other gangland occasions re-created in Billy Wilder's *Some Like It Hot* (1959). Among those present are George Raft, Nehemiah Persoff, Jack Lemmon and Tony Curtis.

Neville Brand as Al Capone in *The Scarface Mob*.

Rod Steiger in *Al Capone*.

that with the cracking of the murder gang, the entire Syndicate had been broken and could be forgotten.' In any event, Americans were soon to be preoccupied by other things: within a week of Lepke's conviction, the Japanese bombed Pearl Harbor. As late as 1951, the year of the Kefauver Committee's televised hearings on organised crime, the confusion of Syndicate and Murder Inc. persisted: '. . . make no mistake about it,' wrote Sid Feder in his introduction to his ghosted memoirs of Burton Turkus, 'Murder, Inc., was and is the national Syndicate'. Although this book was not adapted for the cinema until 1960 (as *Murder Incorporated*, directed by Burt Balaban and Stuart Rosenberg), Turkus himself was clearly the model for the Humphrey Bogart character in *The Enforcer*, which looks at a contract murder squad with hardly more than a faint implication of a larger organisation behind it.

The film industry's experiences with the representatives of organised crime go back to the early 'thirties, even before Bugsy Siegel moved to California in 1937 and started extorting money from film stars by the ingenious expedient of suggesting to them that their next films could be halted by a walk-out of the extras, in whose union local he had gained control. A larger shakedown, already in progress, was more damaging as it was aimed at the industry itself. This operation went back to 1932 and the birth of a partnership in Chicago between a racketeer called Willie Bioff and a union organiser, George E. Browne. Their common interest was the kosher meat business – Bioff had his claws into the butchers while Browne was supplementing his regular income by organising the chicken-dealers. But it was Browne's main area of operation that seemed to offer a big future for the pair; he was business agent of Local 2 of the International Alliance of Theatrical Stage Employees (IATSE), the union which included movie-projectionists. As a springboard to the big time, Local 2 had a serious defect: over half its 400 members were unemployed. The ingenious pair started by organising a soup-kitchen for their members, modestly lining their pockets along the way with donations provided by visiting celebrities.

Their first move against the industry came in 1934, when they went to the most powerful showbusiness figure in Chicago, Barney Balaban, head of the Balaban & Katz which was part of the then bankrupt Paramount. (Balaban, the father of Burt Balaban, became President of Paramount in a reorganisation the following year.) Going in with a demand that a pay cut dealt out to Balaban & Katz's IATSE employees in 1929 should be restored, Bioff and Browne were offered the $7,500 which they mentioned it was costing to run the soup-kitchen. The action thereafter was later recounted by an unrepentant Bioff having his day in court prior to completing a rather longer period in prison: 'I figured right then I might as well kill a sheep as a lamb. Barney turned out to be a lamb. When he agreed to our suggestion, I knew we had him. I told him his contribution would have

subsequent erosion of its ethnic isolationism with the removal of the Mustache Petes by Luciano's men. From 1934, then, the United States had a coast-to-coast Syndicate controlling every facet of crime worthy of large-scale management, and to take care of any killings that were needed in the line of business, the Syndicate had its contract execution department under Louis 'Lepke' Buchalter.

The conviction of Luciano on sixty-two counts of extortion and compulsory prostitution and his sentence of thirty to fifty years did little to expose his role in the larger scheme of things criminal. A lot more came out through the efforts of Assistant District Attorney Burton Turkus and some marathon singing by an entirely unrepentant Syndicate gorilla called Abe 'Kid Twist' Reles. A train of due processes was set in motion starting with the trial in May 1940 of a couple of trigger-men known as Happy Maione and Frank 'Dasher' Abbandando and ending with the execution of Lepke and a couple of his aides in March 1944, more than two years after their conviction. The grisly stories that emerged in the courtrooms induced shock rather than comprehension. According to Hank Messick: 'The public, getting its information from the press which, in turn, depended on public officials, confused the enforcement arm of the Syndicate with the Syndicate itself, and Murder, Inc. came to mean the entire apparatus. . . . Thus it was assumed

In pre-war movies, corrupt politics were often dealt with as comedy. Akim Tamiroff and Brian Donlevy in Preston Sturges's *The Great McGinty* (1940).

Opposite: Peter Falk as Abe 'Kid Twist' Reles in *Murder Incorporated.*

to be $50,000 unless he wanted real trouble. By that I meant we would pull his projectionists out of the theatres. He was appalled, but we turned on the heat. He finally agreed to pay us $20,000. The restoration of the pay cut was forgotten. We were not interested in that then or at any other time. We didn't care whether wages were reduced or raised. We were interested only in getting the dough, and we didn't care how we got it.'

The joint where they celebrated was controlled by the Capone gang, with the result that they found themselves splitting fifty-fifty with the Mafia. But the offer they could not refuse was to take them on to bigger things. The first of these was the presidency of IATSE as a whole for Browne. Although he had been defeated in 1932, he now had connections which were so conspicuously in evidence at the IATSE convention in Louisville in June 1934 that no votes at all were cast against him. With mob backing, Browne and Bioff, now his 'personal representative' and the real boss of the union, went back to work on the Chicago exhibitors to the tune of $100,000, of which $60,000 came from Balaban & Katz and $30,000 from Warners. The pitch this time had been that each movie-house should have two projectionists rather than one in its booth, and as always it seemed cheaper to pay the extortion than improve the lot of the

Murder Incorporated.

Humphrey Bogart as the Assistant DA tries to coax his main witness back to safety in *The Enforcer*.

employees. After this success, the mob's cut was increased to 75 per cent and the insatiable duo ranged far and wide selling the industrial equivalent of protection, 'strike prevention insurance', in which the premiums tended to be substantial – as much as $150,000 in 1935 for the Loew's chain in New York. Deployment of Syndicate muscle also persuaded the studio heads via a large-scale closure of cinemas to give IATSE jurisdiction over labour in Hollywood studios where the union had previously been weak. In 1936, Bioff visited Nicholas Schenck, the head of Loew's which owned MGM, and the industry's representative in union negotiations. Out of this meeting, at which a horrified Schenck learned that Bioff expected to extract $2,000,000 from Hollywood, came an eventual agreement that the majors would pay $50,000 a year and the minor studios half that amount. The only notable refusal came from the indomitable Harry Cohn, the undisputed dictator at Columbia, which did not have a chain of theatres to make it vulnerable. According to Malcolm Johnson in his book 'Crime on the Waterfronts', 'A first payment of $75,000 in cash was made to Bioff and Browne in a room in the Hotel Warwick, New York. Schenck brought $50,000 and Kent [Sidney Kent, president of Twentieth Century-Fox] $25,000. Bioff and Browne dumped the money on a bed and carefully counted it, while Schenck and Kent watched, squirming.'

This bizarre scene, with two of the most powerful men in the film industry handing over an extortion payment to a pair of mob-controlled hoodlums, led to Bioff accumulating a personal fortune of some $100,000 with which he wished to buy a ranch. His effort to turn cash into real estate without interesting the tax authorities, a primitive attempt at what is these days called 'laundering', brought about his downfall. He enlisted the aid of Nicholas Schenck's brother Joseph, who was Chairman of Twentieth Century-Fox, and Joe Schenck's nephew Arthur Stebbins. The incriminating cash was exchanged for a $100,000 cheque from Stebbins and the deal was recorded as a loan to Bioff guaranteed by Schenck. The unexpected result was that instead of Bioff being investigated Schenck was, for apparently having

Humphrey Bogart and his colleagues in *The Enforcer* survey the collection of Murder Inc victims' shoes after the dragging of the swamp used by the squad's contract undertaker as a graveyard.

Humphrey Bogart in *The Enforcer* tries to find the one surviving witness before the hit men reach her.

149

Cop Robert Mitchum and gangster Robert Ryan in *The Racket*.

failed to declare $100,000 of income. Finding himself with a three-year jail sentence for tax evasion, he offered evidence against the two Bs and thus got his term reduced to a year and a day for perjury. He served only four months before going straight back to being Chairman of Fox. The indictments against Bioff and Browne resulted in sentences respectively of ten and eight years and fines of $20,000 and $10,000. This took second place in the newspaper headlines of 12 November 1941 to the mysterious fall of Burton Turkus's star canary, Kid Twist Reles, from the window of a heavily guarded room on the sixth floor of the Half Moon Hotel in Coney Island.

Once convicted, Bioff and Browne told all, and a clutch of Chicago mafiosi were indicted on charges which included the extortion of over $2,500,000 from the film producers and the union members. Among them were Al Capone's first cousin, Frank 'The Enforcer' Nitti, who committed suicide before the trial, and a couple of Capone's ex-bodyguards, Louis Campagna and Phil D'Andrea. Bioff was the star witness at the trial. His story included suggestions of political corruption and a handful of killings, the most colourful victim of which was a figure called Fred 'Bugs' Blacker whose nickname came from his trick of scattering bedbugs in theatres with uncooperative owners. Bioff's career ended on 4 November 1955 when he started his car outside his home in Phoenix, Arizona, and went out with a bang.

It is, then, an established fact that at least from 1936 to the early 'forties, most of the Hollywood studios and the theatres showing their products were paying extortion money to representatives of the Syndicate. Even Warner Brothers, the most crusading of the studios, was paying off. Even without the film industry's particular vulnerability to the attentions of the mob, the degree to which the movies might have been expected to expose organised crime would have been unlikely to exceed the consensus of public opinion at any time, and the consensus up to 1950 had not really accepted the idea of crime organised as a business on a

national scale. After all, J. Edgar Hoover, who as head of the FBI should have been the nation's leading authority on the subject, did not accept that there was a National Crime Syndicate until years after the Kefauver hearings had made the conclusion unavoidable.

The idea of locally organised crime with police and politicians hooked in to its operations was certainly evident in some 'thirties movies. Crime as a form of business – illegal business, but business none the less – was also a theme to be found in such films as *Bullets or Ballots*. The same picture comes across in the occasional 'forties film title: *Larceny Inc* (1942), *Crime Inc* (1945) and even *Dick Tracy vs Crime Inc* (1941). The significance of the Kefauver hearings was not just that they uncovered a stack of new information, identified some of the major heavies in the American underworld and blew the whistle on the scale of involvement between the worlds of business, politics and crime. All this they did, but they also constituted a media event, gaining much of their impact from the fact that the proceedings were televised, an early demonstration of the unprecedented weight with which testimony was endowed by the television cameras. Although organised crime was quickly outgunned in the media by the Red Menace as expounded by Senator McCarthy, the hearings stimulated public interest temporarily. It is possibly significant that Burton Turkus did not see fit to ask Sid Feder to help him write his story until 1950 – it was completed in 1951 – although the events were ten years in the past and Buchalter had been executed in 1944.

The Enforcer (1951) has its direction credited to Bretaigne Windust, although it appears that much of it was directed by Raoul Walsh. In Britain, it was called *Murder Inc*, but it is neither an adaptation of the Turkus/Feder book nor a recounting of the same events. Indeed, the liquidation squad it depicts is never referred to as Murder Inc., just as, twenty years later, the film of *The Godfather* never used the word 'Mafia' to describe the club to which the men of the Corleone family belonged. The events and characters may be entirely fictitious, but Martin Rackin's story and screenplay uses an even more generous measure of modified factual material than most of the 'thirties crime movies. Although the film has the general iconography of gangster movies to draw upon, it has clearly been made with the awareness that as far as the specifics of the enforcement business are concerned, it is on its own. In opening up a new subject area for the movies, its treatment had a strong didactic element which was on the whole skilfully assimilated into the narrative.

Even the basic vocabulary is defined for us: the first time that Assistant DA Martin Ferguson (Bogart) and his assistants hear the words 'hit' and 'contract' from James 'Duke' Molloy, they are baffled. Molloy has stumbled into a police station to recount incoherently that they had made him kill his girl – he had to kill her – it was a hit – Babe, Philadelphia and

Marlon Brando in *On the Waterfront* with Lee J. Cobb (*left*), Eva Marie Saint (*below*) and Rod Steiger (*bottom*).

After Lee Marvin has scalded Gloria Grahame's face with the coffee in *The Big Heat*.

Smiley made him – he told her it wouldn't hurt and it didn't. Before Ferguson can get him to decipher the unfamiliar terminology, Molloy has hanged himself in his cell.

As Philadelphia has got himself packed back to an asylum and Smiley Schultz comes to light when his body is discovered to be the blockage that is making a heating furnace smoke, the explanations are provided by Big Babe (Zero Mostel). We learn with Ferguson the meaning of a contract and a hit. The script is always careful to translate any new pieces of underworld jargon: describing Molloy as a schlammer, Babe adds the explanation 'strong-arm man'. From a very scared Babe, a relative newcomer to the business, Ferguson elicits a description of the office run by Rico (Ted De Corsia) in a room behind Olga's lunch-stand.

This joint exemplifies the relationship of *The*

Lee Van Cleef, Jean Wallace and Earl Holliman in *The Big Combo*.

Enforcer to Turkus's documentary narrative: the meeting-place for such gorillas as Reles, Abbandando, Happy Maione and Pittsburgh Phil (these last two names are mutated into Smiley and Philadelphia for the film) was a twenty-four-hour candy-store known as Midnight Rose's under the El at the intersection of Saratoga and Livonia avenues in the Brownsville area of New York.

The factual inspiration is most obvious in the details of the squad's activities as these emerge and in the opening of the film with the fantastic precautions being taken by the police to stop their witness being reached by assassins. Although Rico's death is the result of an irrational impulse to flee and Reles's was a mystery as he was being guarded by half a dozen of New York's finest in a locked suite, both deaths were by falling a number of storeys (and the official report on Reles's demise attributed it to a miscalculated attempt to escape by climbing down to a recently vacated room on the floor below).

Even though the film is not specific about Murder Inc.'s customers, it lays out with admirable clarity the service offered and the rationale behind it. It also suggests the scale of operations – after the squad's regular undertaker has shown the DA's men the marsh he has been using for interments, there is a shot of the police forensic laboratory which includes a large collection of shoes that have been fished out with the remains of their occupants.

The film's equivalent of Louis 'Lepke' Buchalter is Mendoza (Everett Sloane) who had, as Rico says, quite an idea – a lunatic idea, but it worked. Rico has given himself up to Ferguson at a rendezvous on a deserted waterfront pier after he has seen his associates eliminated by out-of-town assassins – Herman and BJ from Kansas City – in a scene that recalls the whole-sale slaughter of potential witnesses, even close colleagues, ordained by Buchalter during the Big Heat before his surrender in 1939.

Rico's recollections start with him beating up Mendoza who reacts with admiration: 'I've been gone over by experts but you're the best. I think I can use a guy like you. Come on, I'll buy you a cup of coffee if I've got a dime left.' Over coffee, Mendoza calmly announces that he is a great man who has come too late because all the rackets are sewn up. However, he has a new racket – something no one has thought of before: to service people with a killer who has got no motive. After all, it is the motive that usually leads the cops to the murderer. Then Mendoza, whom Rico describes as having nerves like steel, tells him, 'This is my first contract. I'm getting five hundred bucks.' And he walks over and knifes the café-owner, and exits coolly with a very nervous Rico after the hit had been observed by a pair of arriving customers.

The Enforcer establishes the principles of the apparently motiveless contract killing and of the total elimination of witnesses. The scene of the first contract explains the death of the girl killed by Molloy and the rubbing out of a cab-driver and a barber by Rico – the usual pattern of the film is to show the terror and then get to the reasons in the company of the detec-

Cornel Wilde and Jay Adler in *The Big Combo*.

tives on the case. The cab-driver and his daughter were, apart from Rico, the only wit-nesses of Mendoza's first contract, the only one on which he made the hit himself. The driver has recognised Mendoza who, long after the murder, has taken a ride in his cab; the barber has been forced to help in the murder of the driver – Rico briefs the barber to put hot towels on the man's face for his shave, 'start to strop the razor – then I take over'. The one question which is never answered is why any-one would want the owner of a diner killed.

The story of the film is mainly told in two layers of flashback after Ferguson's case against Mendoza (like Turkus's against Bugsy Siegel) had gone out the window with his chief witness. Mendoza's lawyers will go to court in the morning and get a dismissal – Ferguson

Cornel Wilde and Helen Stanton in *The Big Combo*.

John Payne in *The Boss*.

Mickey Rooney as a racket boss in Charles Haas's *The Big Operator* (1959).

could not even get him thirty days. He goes back over the evidence 'the way it came to us from that first crazy day', and there is a flashback to Molloy giving himself up. As Ferguson and his assistant review the evidence looking for a new angle, we get further flashbacks as Big Babe and the others culminating in Rico tell their stories. At the end, Ferguson has made no progress; he goes down to the cells and presents Mendoza with the photographs of his victims. The two men independently realise that one witness still survives: the girl Molloy fell in love with and was made to murder was the wrong girl. The finger had not pointed out the cab-driver's blonde daughter but her dark-eyed brunette flat-mate. Herman and BJ learn that their boss wants a contract done straight away. Using the loudspeaker on the outside of a record store, Ferguson alerts the girl and just manages to save her: 'You've got a date in court. I want to see that smile fade on Mendoza's face when he looks into these big blue eyes again.'

The Enforcer suggests the existence of an organisation beyond Murder Inc. itself only in odd details, most overtly when the two killers arrive at the squad's rural hide-out and say 'Everything comes out of Kansas City now. You don't have to worry – you'll be taken care of' (which they are with finality by the two gunmen). Otherwise the larger context exists only in the fact that the contracts which Mendoza telephones to Rico have to come from somewhere, and Rico's killers provide only one part of the arrangement. About one contract, Rico says that the finger does not speak much English and gets the reply 'He can point, can't he?' There are other indications, too, that this is not just a self-contained gang at the beginning and end of the movie when all of its members are either dead or in custody: the snipers equipped with telescopic sights waiting on a rooftop for the chance of getting a shot at Rico, and the speed with which a closely guarded Mendoza can put out a contract on the girl whose evidence could send him to the electric chair.

The film implies a realisation, which seems to have been new in the movies, that the fight against crime had grown into a very different game: no longer could it be seen just as a matter of dealing out just deserts for the heavies. With a nationwide syndicate organising crime, wiping out one bunch of hoodlums would simply result in the hiring of some more. The focus in *The Enforcer* and some of the other films about organised crime made in the first half of the 'fifties was on witnesses, on the problems of finding people who could testify and then on keeping them alive to do so. The last piece of action in *The Enforcer* may be a gun battle, but only minor heavies are involved, and the point of the sequence is not that Ferguson manages to shoot Herman and BJ but that the girl can now give evidence which will convict the key executive rather than the hired executioners.

Richard Fleischer's *The Narrow Margin*, made in the following year, develops a similar theme in the form of a straightforward and bril-

liantly effective thriller. Where *The Enforcer*, breaking new cinematic ground, was built round the revelation of the contract murder business, *The Narrow Margin* is able to assume that the exercise of transporting a gangster's widow across the country to testify at a Federal Grand Jury hearing will have to contend with a criminal organisation which has limitless resources and total determination to prevent the witness from talking.

The difficulty of finding people to speak out against the mobsters, and their vulnerability if they do speak or even might speak are themes that turn up again in Fritz Lang's *The Big Heat* (1953) and Elia Kazan's *On the Waterfront* (1954) and much later in Samuel Fuller's *Underworld USA* (1961), which, like *The Big Heat*, has a policeman – though a more important one – shoot himself rather than testify against the Syndicate.

The interest generated by the Kefauver hearings seems to have led producers to figure that the opportunity might have arrived for a renaissance of the old-fashioned crime picture with Syndicate trimmings – Howard Hughes, who was head of RKO, exhumed a gangster play which he had produced as a movie in 1928 with direction by Lewis Milestone and remade it under the same title, *The Racket*, now with John Cromwell as the director in 1951. Even from across the Atlantic, the inspiration for the remake was noted, as was the age of the material. The 'Monthly Film Bulletin' commented that 'it presumably once presented a credible and exciting picture of gang warfare. Not even the revelations of the Kefauver Committee investigations can prevent this new version from appearing jaded and highly artificial, with an improbably over-simplified view of the crime ring's operation'.

The Racket, starring Robert Mitchum as the cop and Robert Ryan as the hood – by no means a cheapie – was an early arrival in the salvo of post-Kefauver crime movies. A larger number were turned out in 1952, often with direct references to the hearings. Thus, Robert Wise's *The Captive City* ends with the editor of a small-town newspaper going under police protection to testify to the Kefauver Committee, and at a much lower level, a Republic B-feature, *Hoodlum Empire*, directed by Joe Kane, is set round a Congressional Committee investigation into

Nick Mancani (Luther Adler) and his large-scale gambling operations. The 'Monthly Film Bulletin' observed that the framework was 'clearly derived from the Kefauver investigations, and an attempt has been made to reproduce the atmosphere, from the barrage of television cameras to the behaviour of certain witnesses'. The structure, though, had something in common with *The Enforcer* (and was perhaps the inevitable narrative cliché of a cycle based on investigation and testimony). The 'MFB' again: 'the story provides familiar gangster melodramatics and repentances played out in a rigmarole of flashbacks at an adequate, tough "B" picture level of presentation'. In 1953, there was, for example, Lewis Seiler's *The System*, in which a Crime Investigating Committee comes to the town where John Merrick (Frank Lovejoy) has his rackets organised behind a front of legitimate business. In fact, Merrick's operation is only the local branch of the national crime and gambling syndicate called 'The System' in which Mr Big is Marty (Dan Seymour).

Through these and many other films, the public was provided with glimpses of Syndicate techniques and a whole gallery of personnel such as *Finger Man* (1955). *Loan Shark* (1952), directed by Seymour Friedman with a screenplay partly by Martin Rackin, who also wrote the story, had George Raft as a tough ex-con working as an undercover agent for the FBI to expose the ringleaders of a loan-sharking racket that has moved in on the employees of a tyre factory.

Robert Parrish's *The Mob* (1951) introduces Syndicate penetration of the waterfront unions, using established format of the undercover agent movie. The most notable, and certainly the most discussed, movie about this area of organised crime was Elia Kazan's *On the Waterfront* (1954) which has a script by Budd Schulberg suggested by the reportage of Malcolm Johnson, the author of the 1950 book

Left: Vince Edwards finally gets into the hit's home in *Murder by Contract.*

Richard Widmark and Tina Louise in *The Trap.*

'Crime on the Waterfronts' (quoted earlier in this chapter on the cinematic activities of Messrs Bioff and Browne). This is a film which does not invite discussion simply as a genre crime movie; both the complexities of motivation behind it and the controversy aroused by its appearance set it apart from its contemporaries. The ending was attacked by Lindsay Anderson as Fascist, because it set up Marlon Brando as the new strong man of the waterfront. Kazan disagreed totally: 'I thought I knew more about the waterfront than anyone except Budd Schulberg. It wasn't a careless job of research; I was living there, and I learned a lot about the waterfront – and also about politics and elections, which Lindsay Anderson didn't know a goddamned thing about. All he had was this schematic left-wing idea about the ending. There's nothing fascist about the end of the picture.' Considerably more germane than Anderson's comment was the suggestion made, notably by Roger Tailleur in his book on Kazan, that the picture was a defence of the giving of testimony by him and Schulberg before the House Committee on Un-American Activities. Long after the event, again talking in 1971 to Stuart Byron and Martin Rubin, Kazan commented: 'Well, I think it's partly

affected by that, naturally. I went through that thing, and it was painful and difficult and not the thing I'm proudest of in my life, but it's also not something I'm ashamed of. I was affected by that, but it's not the main thing in the film. To say that we made the film as a defence of that just isn't so. Because that's exactly what happened on the waterfront. The story is based on the experiences of a real person: I used to have dinner with him all the time. Schulberg and I went over there while the inquest was going on. And it happens again and again. It happens at all these Mafia trials. Silence, silence, silence.'

As a genre movie, *On the Waterfront* contributed a notable new figure to the iconography of crime in the shape of the brutally corrupt but in some respects almost paternalistic union boss, Johnny Friendly (Lee J. Cobb). According to John M. Smith, 'Friendly's dominant position is based on a massive egotism and is an impressive personal achievement of which he is proud: he has a taste for grandeur and despises pettiness, and we haven't got the film right if we don't grant his splendour as well as his tawdriness.'

The other notable film on union corruption dealt with another celebrated field for Syndicate activities: the garment workers' unions. *The Garment Center* (1957), called *The Garment Jungle* in Britain, was largely directed by Robert Aldrich but credited to Vincent Sherman who took over after disagreements when the picture was nearly finished and was presumably responsible for the few scenes which are clearly out of place in an otherwise excellent piece of work. This time Lee J. Cobb was on the management side and paying protection money to Richard Boone; urged on by his clean-limbed son (Kerwin Matthews), Cobb eventually saw sense, refused to pay, and came to an untimely end.

These union movies were among the few that were able to deal with specific areas of Syndicate operations. Hollywood in the early 'fifties had a problem with crime movies that it had not had in the 'thirties when the ramifications of the illegal liquor business provided not just a useful factual background but one that could be dealt with overtly. As subjects for racketeering dramas, artichokes, olive oil or mozzarella cheese and any of the innumerable consumer goods on which the Mafia took a levy would probably (and wrongly) have seemed like small-time operations of little general interest. Two other staple sources of income for the Syndicate were unmentionable in the early 'fifties because of the Hays Code: narcotics could be referred to only in circumlocutions until well after 1955 and Otto Preminger's Code-breaking operations in *The Man with the Golden Arm*; prostitution was off the menu as an overt topic for even longer. The mentionable activity was gambling, which was illegal in most states of the Union, and the early Syndicate movies tend to describe its operations as crime and gambling, leaving the audience to guess what was meant by crime.

Whether it was because the crimes by which

the heavies were profiting could not be detailed, or because of a socially cleansing function that the media of communication from newspapers and television to theatre and novels have repeatedly taken upon themselves in the United States, the theme that runs most consistently through crime movies from *The Racket* in 1951 to *Underworld USA* in 1961 is not the law-breaking itself but the corruption that comes with it. The crime movies of the 'thirties, notably *Bullets or Ballots*, recognised that the politicians, administrators and law-enforcement officers were not immune from enticement or forcing into collaboration with the racketeers. What was new in the 'fifties was the consistent picture in film after film of the permeation at every echelon of the civil administration by corruption and of the apathy on the part of the public which permitted this. Lawrence Alloway quotes a line uttered in Jack Arnold's *Man in the Shadow* (1957) by Jeff Chandler as the Sheriff investigating a millionaire rancher when he is warned by the local citizens that he is killing their town: 'This isn't a town, it's a trained dog act.'

In *The Racket*, the heavy, Nick Scanlon (Robert Ryan), counts at his trial on the help of the prosecuting attorney, a politician in the pay of the local Syndicate's ultimate leader, the unseen figure referred to as The Old Man – another recurring piece of imagery in Syndicate movies: the invisible, unreachable personification of complete, evil power, who turns up, for instance as The Man Upstairs in *On the Water-front*. Scanlon's old-fashioned use of brutality and murder have, however, made him something of a liability to the Syndicate and he is

double-crossed by the lawyer.

The Captive City (1952) has its journalist hero (John Forsythe) discovering that the Police Chief in the small town where he has settled appears to be controlled by a racketeer called Sirak who forms part of a larger network of inter-State criminal conspiracy. The apathy of the citizenry is not shattered even when it emerges that the picture is more complicated and even less savoury than it first appeared:

Murder Incorporated.

Peter Breck as the reporter in *Shock Corridor* being restrained by two male nurses.

157

Sirak is only a minor figure in the local crime
syndicate which is actually organised by the
Mayor, members of the Town Council, the
Police Chief and a gangster on the lam.

No less stark in its picture of municipal
corruption is *The Big Heat*, made in the following year. This starts with a man shooting himself – he is later identified as the cop in charge of
records. The man's wife (Jeanette Nolan) comes
downstairs to find her husband's body. On the
desk in front of him is his badge and a letter
to the District Attorney. She reads cursorily
through the many pages of this document and
makes a telephone call, asking for 'Mr Lagana
– tell him it's Tom Duncan's widow.' Mike
Lagana (Alexander Scourby), the town's Syndicate boss, immediately realises that Bertha
Duncan has reacted to her bereavement with
a desire to take her husband's place on the
payroll. 'Yes, of course we will get together,'
Lagana reassures her, 'but now I suggest you
call the police immediately.' No sooner has he
put down the telephone and had his cigarette
lit by a henchman than he calls his second in
command, Vince Stone (Lee Marvin) whose job
is to tidy away details like Duncan's mistress
who has been talking to the police. Vince is not
a nice person: the girl's body is thrown from a
car and bears the marks of beating and torture.
The police surgeon opines that 'pretty definitely
it was psychopathic – you saw those cigarette
burns on her body'. 'Yes, every one of them,'
replies Dave Bannion (Glenn Ford), the detective assigned to the case. Lagana, on the other
hand, has a smoothly respectable life style in a
mansion guarded by ten cops.('Well, he kind of
runs things around here. That's no secret.')
The room in which Lagana is confronted by
Bannion has a picture of Lagana's mother, 'a
great old lady', over the fireplace, and the house
is given over to a party for his daughter. The
family man is affronted that Bannion should
burst in to question him about a murder – he has

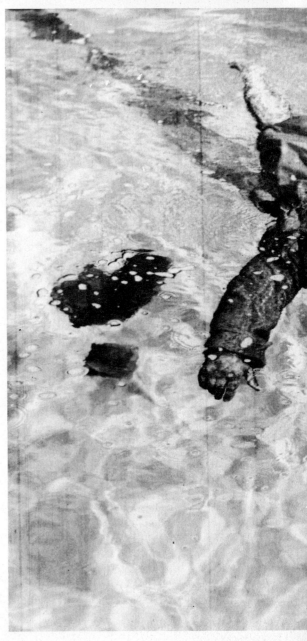

got an office for dealing with this kind of thing – this is his home, and he does not want dirt tracked in. Bannion (who is known in the police department as 'a corn-stepper by instinct') opines that he could not plant enough flowers round this house to kill the smell.

Bannion is ordered repeatedly to lay off by his lieutenant ('that leaning tower of jelly,' Bannion calls him), whose timidity in the face of being 'pressured from upstairs' is partly because he has only a few years to serve before retirement. The pressure is hardly surprising as the Police Commissioner seems to be a regular participant at card-games in Vince Stone's apartment. He is even present at the film's most famous scene when Vince punishes his girl friend Debbie (Gloria Grahame) for talking to Bannion by throwing a flask of boiling coffee at her face. Debbie is, outside the rather oversold togetherness of the Bannion household, the most sympathetic character in the picture, a spontaneously friendly and surprisingly mischievous good-time girl. She tells Bannion 'I've been rich and I've been poor, and,

Richard Rust as Gus, Paul Dubov and Cliff Robertson in *Underworld USA*.

believe me, rich is better.'

Her disfigurement is one of Stone's mistakes. Previously he has had a bomb planted in Bannion's car, and succeeded in killing the detective's wife. As a result, Bannion, obsessed with vengeance, walks out of the police department and sets out to get Stone and Lagana unrestrained by the niceties of police technique and the influence brought to bear on his

The body of Robert Emhardt as Earl Connors, the chief of National Projects, floating in the swimming-pool of the penthouse executive suite in *Underworld USA*.

159

Johnny Cool with Marc Lawrence as the exiled Syndicate boss (*above*) and Henry Silva as Johnny Cool (*right*).

superior. Although he eventually accepts help even from the lieutenant, the feeling conveyed by the film is deeply pessimistic: it is only Bannion's violent abandonment of the restraints imposed on him by the very organisation entrusted with keeping the law that produces a situation in which the gangsters can be defeated. An alternative view is expressed by Tom Flinn about *The Big Heat* and another Syndicate movie, Joseph H. Lewis's *The Big Combo* (1955): in spite of their apparent willingness 'to treat the subject of organised crime realistically, neither film offered anything approaching a practical method for combating criminal organisations. Perhaps the greatest distortion in both films is the concept that organised crime can be defeated by the activities of one determined or, depending on your point of view, demented individual.' But these films were making their diagnoses at a time when the leading specialist at the FBI believed the body politic to be infected with an

entirely different disease, the Red Menace. It is unreasonable to expect these movies also to take on the job of writing out an effective prescription. It is worth repeating that no other major film industry has even approached Hollywood in drawing attention to a nation's ills.

Civic corruption continued to be dealt with in movies up to the start of the 'sixties, and made a come-back with the police cycle that started in 1968 – in Don Siegel's *Madigan* and Gordon Douglas's *The Detective*, James Whitmore and Ralph Meeker respectively were taking pay-offs from some tentacle of the Syndicate. Among the 'fifties movies, a couple from 1956, Byron Haskin's *The Boss* and Allan Dwan's *Slightly Scarlet*, both cast John Payne as the gangster boss of a city, though Dwan's movie makes Payne's exploits in taking over the town definitely secondary to the relationship of nutty, nymphomaniac Arlene Dahl and her sane, greedy, unsympathetic sister Rhonda Fleming, an area in which the picture had to operate within Code limitations so that it was, in Dwan's words, 'a handcuff job'.

The usual locale for civic-corruption movies was a generalised town; it could be small or large, but unless it was New York or Los Angeles (which encompassed a wide enough range of administrative units to allow a high degree of anonymity to the setting), the corrupt town was usually not identified. It might take its characteristics from Cleveland or Detroit, Newport, Kentucky or Saratoga Springs, NY, but it was not any of these places. One exception to this was Phil Karlson's *Phenix City Story* (1955). Phenix City, Alabama, was, according to Hank Messick, one of the places where illegal gambling continued during the Second World War: 'cheap bust-out joints . . . stayed open to help servicemen spend their money.' Tom Flinn notes that the documentary basis for the film was the career of Alabama's Attorney-General Patterson; he describes the film (which is the gap in my crime movie viewing that I most regret) as 'one of the finest examples of the genre, and one of the few films to examine the spread of gangster domination from the big cities to the often easier to control small towns'. The specificity of the film is stressed in Lawrence Alloway's description of its opening: it 'begins with a documentary coverage of the city including interviews with the inhabitants; then there is a studio sequence in which a girl in a bar sings about the sinful city; and finally the actors move into the real locations'. The film's hero, John Patterson (Richard Kiley), is a young lawyer who has just returned from military service to Phenix City which is a Syndicate-controlled centre for gambling and prostitution – the film's advertising campaign used the slogan Sin City USA, although the 'Monthly Film Bulletin' observed (possibly because the British release version had lost some footage to the censor) that it had little more to show in the way of sin than a few sleazy bars. Patterson is shocked not just by the conditions in the town but also by the action of law-abiding citizens who are forming vigilante organisations. To get the power to use the law to fight the Syndicate, he persuades his father (John McIntire) to run for election as State Attorney-General. The savagery of the campaign culminates in the murder of Patterson Sr soon after he has won. A witness is murdered and eventually Patterson has to get the Governor to call in the state troopers. With the Syndicate knocked out, Patterson is elected as the new Attorney-General.

Even for a film made at a point in time, the mid 'fifties, which produced a major escalation in screen violence, it appears to have been unusually rough. The 'Monthly Film Bulletin' disapproved: 'for a film whose frequently proclaimed moral is that violence must be met not by force but by the processes of law, *Phenix City Story* contrives to incorporate a sizable amount of elementary brutality'. Making allowances for the liberal film critic's automatic horror at the sight of violence on the screen, one might equally welcome the lack of tasteful restraint here and in such films as *The Big Heat, The Big Combo* and Paul Wendjos's *The Case Against Brooklyn* (1958) as a recognition of the wholesale viciousness involved; in any event, the portrayal was still positively appetising compared to the real thing as described, say, in James Mills's book 'The

Eli Wallach in *The Line Up*.

Prosecutor'.

Among the organised-crime movies of the 'fifties, Norman Panama's *The Trap* (*The Baited Trap* in Britain) was unique in having a rural setting. It offers an extension of the iconography simply by being in colour, unlike the earlier Syndicate movies, and the fact heightens the feeling of invasion of the small community which is near an airstrip that can be

Lee Marvin about to propel John Vernon towards a fall from a great height in *Point Blank*.

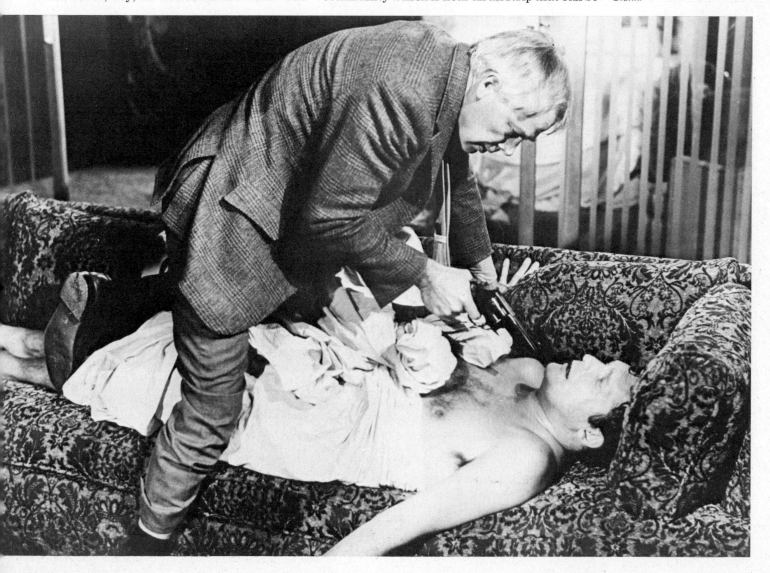

Lee Marvin as the gangster hero of Michael Ritchie's *Prime Cut*.

Charley Varrick. Andy Robinson with Walter Matthau (*right*) and the surprising amount of loot; and (*opposite*) after the Mafia's hit man (Joe Don Baker) has caught up with him.

used for smuggling a Syndicate boss (Lee J. Cobb) out of the country. The aloof figure with dark glasses, seen through the blue-tinted glass of his glossy limousine, jars visually against the straightforward colours and textures of the surroundings. There is another contrast between the well-cut suit of the underworld lawyer (Richard Widmark) who has had the idea of using his birthplace as the exit point for Cobb and the uniform worn by his brother (Earl Holliman) who has stayed at home and become the local Sheriff. These two and the Sheriff's wife (Tina Louise) are the main characters; Cobb acts mainly as a catalyst to the action in which the two brothers in effect change sides. Organised crime was by this time a sufficiently established phenomenon in movies that it could be used confidently as an element in movies that were in no way about it.

On 25 October 1957, Albert Anastasia, who had been the boss of Murder Inc. after the arrest of Buchalter, was having a haircut in the barber-shop of the Hotel Park Sheraton on Seventh Avenue in New York. Two masked men walked straight up to the chair and shot him repeatedly in the head, then walked out again. This and another newsworthy event during the following month, the Mafia convention at Apalachin, NY, which was almost accidentally discovered by a local police sergeant, brought organised crime back into the headlines.

The following year, perhaps for reasons unconnected with these events, saw the arrival of a gangster protagonist who had been around before but had not been examined in such a dispassionate way. As a contract killer, Vince Edwards in Irving Lerner's *Murder by Contract* is totally unlike the doomed, romantic figure personified by Alan Ladd in *This Gun for Hire*. Claude wants to be a contractor – he tells his prospective employer that he has a steady job with fringe benefits but wants to improve himself. He wants to buy a certain house on the Ohio River and on his current salary it would take twenty years. We get some quick glimpses of Claude's early contracts, one of which is executed in a barber-shop; it is not a gun job

like the erasure of Anastasia but a razor job, a technique already practised in the movies by Ted De Corsia in *The Enforcer*. We also see a more sophisticated job in a hospital which is just a matter of turning off a valve and pinching a tube. The treatment throughout is very cool indeed: the replacement of the usual dramatic orchestral score with Perry Botkin Jr's guitar music was surely not just a symptom of the rock-bottom budget (which did not express itself in the B-feature manner of restriction to a few flimsy or borrowed sets but in location shooting done at lightning speed by a brilliant cameraman, Lucien Ballard). The music contributes to the lack of emotion: Claude is not a psychopath but a man doing a job. By the time he arrives in California to do a contract, he is experienced enough to say to the local finger-men that he does not do rush jobs. It may take an hour or a week but that is his deal with the chief. So the fingers find themselves helping him occupy his time with such activities as deep-sea fishing while they get more and more impatient. Does not he want the money? He wants to do a good job – if you do a good job, the money comes. When, three days before the trial that is the reason for the contract, he learns that the hit is a woman, his immediate reaction is to say he has to phone New York and re-negotiate the whole contract. The more understanding of the finger-men guesses that he does not like to damage a woman. But it is not a matter of sex, it is a matter of money. Claude does not like women – they will not stand still, and it is difficult to kill someone who is unpredictable. The witness is also very well guarded, and Claude has to resort to considerable ingenuity. After the failure of his first attempt, he decides that the contract is jinxed

jects. (A related form is adopted in Fuller's next movie, the amazing *Shock Corridor*, in which a journalist gets himself committed to an asylum in order to win a Pulitzer Prize by investigating an unsolved murder that had happened there.)

The most striking feature of *Underworld USA* apart from its impact is the completeness of the identification between the organisation of National Syndicates and that of any other big business. Beside the swimming-pool in the penthouse executive offices, the head of the corporation, Earl Connors (Robert Emhardt) holds a meeting of the departmental heads. He instructs Gela, the narcotics man, to put more field-men to work around the schools. He asks Gunther, who deals with the union interests, why they have made no headway with the longshoremen. Smith, who controls prostitution, is informed that he showed a loss last month. Having covered the specific points on his agenda, Connors finishes in true executive style with a pep talk to all three: 'You think I like sitting on you like this? I hate it. But it's got to be done if we're to stay on top.'

Even Tolly, who is not the sort of delinquent to fit in with the constraints of corporate existence, understands the situation perfectly. Presenting Gela with a pack of narcotics that he has taken from a hiding-place maintained by the narcotics division of National Projects, he refuses payment, telling him, 'I'd like a future with your organisation. I've often wanted security.'

The film draws on a variety of early 'fifties reference points: the man to whom Tolly reports when it suits his purpose is Driscoll, the chief of a Federal Crime Committee, who is making no headway because intimidation, bribery and murder have taken care of the potential witnesses. But the ultimate reason for the Syndicate's success is the apathy of the public, and the film's energies are directed in an attack on its audience. V. F. Perkins has pinpointed the film's attitude to its public: 'Gullible, apathetic and gutless, the American people have allowed "the punks" to take office.' At the end of his pool-side meeting Connors tells his colleagues: 'There'll always be guys like Driscoll and there'll always be guys like us. As long as we keep books and subscribe to charities, we'll win the war. We always have.'

The failure of Driscoll's efforts until the Syndicate is cracked open by obsessively vengeful Tolly recalls the pessimism of films like *The Big Heat*, but with the difference that the source of desperate energy is not in the least interested in restoring the rule of law. As soon as the third of his father's killers is dead, Tolly wants only to leave National Projects behind, although Driscoll tells him: 'You'll never be able to start from scratch unless you help us put Connors away.' He is only brought to realise this by the arrival of Gus (Richard Rust), the hit man on the staff of National Projects, with the news that they have located a potential witness for Driscoll. Gus gives Tolly a gun: Connors wants Gus to break him in

and wants to return east. His local contacts, though, have instructions to kill him if he fails to complete the job. Instead he kills them and makes another attempt at the job, a very professional effort using a culvert he has discovered by searching through the Hall of Records. When he gets to the hit, he cannot bring himself to strangle her although there is nothing to stop him. He is shot as he tries to crawl away along the drain. The jinxed contract aspect and Claude's final inability to do the job are the least interesting (and the least convincing) parts of the film. Where it breaks new ground is in the presentation of Claude as a man who sees his position in much the same light as his previous and less remunerative employment as an expert comptometer operator at $76.20 a week before taxes. The old image of the hoodlum has gone: he is a technician working for a business corporation.

The Syndicate as a business, which is only hinted at in *Murder by Contract*, becomes a much clearer concept in later pictures including Samuel Fuller's *Underworld USA* (1961) and John Boorman's *Point Blank* (1967). In Fuller's movie, the Syndicate is called National Projects, a corporation which has 'a legitimate business façade from the basement up to the penthouse executive offices'. *Underworld USA* is in many ways as pivotal a crime movie as *The Roaring Twenties*, *High Sierra*, *White Heat* and *The Enforcer* were in their days. It differs obviously in its low budget and relative lack of success, and in the absence of Raoul Walsh and Humphrey Bogart. Curiously enough, at least the title of the film had its origin in a 'Saturday Evening Post' serial which Bogart bought for his Santana company and which was acquired by Ray Stark for Columbia from Bogart's estate. According to Fuller, his script has nothing to do with the serial, but possibly the age of the project's origins helps explain the way it summarises the iconography of Syndicate movies that had been built up over the decade since *The Enforcer*. Its form is even older than that: it is a variant on the undercover-agent movie, though Tolly Devlin (Cliff Robertson) is an ex-convict who infiltrates National Projects out of motives of revenge. When he was a child, his father was beaten to death by four men, the three survivors of whom are now departmental heads at National Pro-

by letting him wipe out the man, his wife and child.

Gus, unlike Tolly, is not at all psychopathic. He is, as Perkins points out, all the more chilling because he kills without enjoyment. Showing Tolly over the National Projects skyscraper, Gus has told him about the swimming-pool on the roof 'for the bigwigs and underprivileged kids. The Chamber of Commerce gave us a plaque . . . I even acted as a lifeguard for the kids one day. I liked that.' Later we see him having a friendly chat with a small girl and giving her gum – clearly he likes kids, but this child is the daughter of Driscoll's witness. Gus makes a telephone call and is ordered to kill her. Without hesitation, he puts on his dark glasses, gets into his car and runs her down.

Gus doesn't even have the hang-ups over physical fitness and cleanliness which provided suggestions in *Murder by Contract* that perhaps Claude might be in some way unbalanced. He is the forerunner of the equally smooth executive-like killers who appear in later 'sixties crime movies. In William Asher's *Johnny Cool* (1963), the killer is the central figure in a story based on the fictional premise that a Sicilian who is clearly meant to represent Salvatore Giuliano has only appeared to be shot down in his native land as cover for him to be spirited away to work as a killer in America for an exiled Mafia boss. The bulk of the film is devoted to his progress across America coolly rubbing out a series of well-known character actors.

Don Siegel's *The Killers* was made for television in 1964 but propelled into the cinemas by its violence which made it unsuitable for the prime-time audience. Distantly inspired by Ernest Hemingway's short story and Robert Siodmak's 1946 film, it begins with two dapper killers, Charlie (Lee Marvin) and Lee (Clu Gulager), on a contract; they go to a school for blind children and shoot one of the teachers (John Cassavetes), who troubles Charlie by showing little interest in survival. Lawrence Alloway has pointed out that the ensuing investigation by Charlie of the victim's background develops an idea that had been implicit in an early Siegel movie *The Line Up* (1958) in which a very much weirder pair of killers went around San Francisco tracking down a list of people who have unwittingly been used to carry heroin into the country. In that picture, Eli Wallach, who actually does the killing, is so

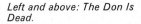

Left and above: The Don Is Dead.

Opposite: The Valachi Papers.

167

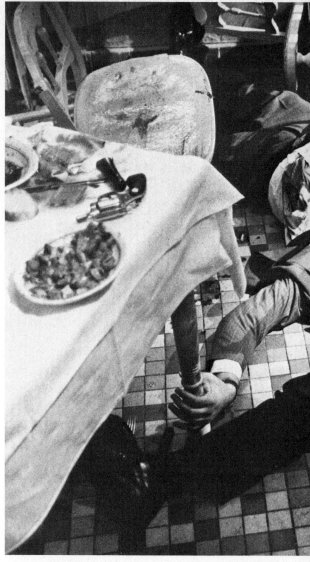

Above and *right:* two scenes from *Honor Thy Father* with (*above*) Joseph Bologna as Bill Bonanno and Raf Vallone as his father.

nerveless as to be virtually a zombie; he is accompanied everywhere by his fastidious elderly mentor, Robert Keith, who tries to give him refinement or at least teach him the correct use of English.

If Gus in *Underworld USA* is the archetype of professional killers seen since on screens of all dimensions, the business image of National Projects has become a standard cinematic concept of organised crime, appearing, for instance, in *Point Blank*, in which Lee Marvin cuts a path of destruction through the smoothly organised operations of a Syndicate staffed by prosperous executives emitting an air of impeccable respectability.

Back in the 'fifties, a repeated pattern in crime movies (and, for that matter, in westerns) pitted a lone hero against an organisation. He could be cop or a DA or a crusading journalist. He could be idealistic or stubborn or crazy with hate and lusting for revenge. In some way or other, though, his activities were characteristically blessed with legality or at least with some sort of moral sanction for any brutality that he might use. Since the late 'fifties, the emphasis has changed and the loner is likely himself to be a criminal. In the 'seventies, the lone criminal even stands a chance of ending the film having derived some positive advantage like a very large sum of money from behaviour which may have included grand larceny and first degree murder. The Syndicate, by combining crime with the dehumanising qualities of big business, is irredeemably repellent where individual crime may at least be endowed with the joys of anarchy or appear as an attack on the establishment. *Charley Varrick* and *The Getaway* are representatives of an as yet unresolved tendency in films, moving perhaps towards a feeling that there are things worse than breaking the law, or offering a picture of a world of such Darwinian ferocity that survival is in itself an achievement worthy of reward.

In Sam Peckinpah's *The Getaway* (1972), the bank-robber McCoy (Steve McQueen) and his wife (Ali MacGraw) escape with the money in which the man who has set up the robbery has not planned for McCoy to share. The corrupt businessman (Ben Johnson) who has power enough over the parole board to get McCoy out whenever he likes is a sufficiently evil figure to leave the McCoys as the most sympathetic characters around. In *The Getaway*, McCoy takes the money first from a bank and then from the man who had been planning to use his skills and then do away with him. Walter Matthau in Don Siegel's *Charley Varrick* (1973) also robs a bank, a job which results in a number of deaths including that of his wife, the driver of the getaway car. What was expected to be a small-time robbery and is presented as such by the bank produces $750,000. The explanation is that the money is Mafia money, which means that Varrick and his young helper Harman (Andy Robinson) are hunted men. Harman, who only wants to have a good time with the money, soon gets wiped out but Varrick, thanks to his guile and his skill as a stunt pilot, survives. In both these films, pursuit by the police takes second place as a threat to pursuit by brutal heavies represented in *The Getaway* by Rudy (Al Lettieri) and in *Charley Varrick* by Molly (Joe Don Baker).

It is perhaps an iconographical sign of the times that a Syndicate which is ethnically

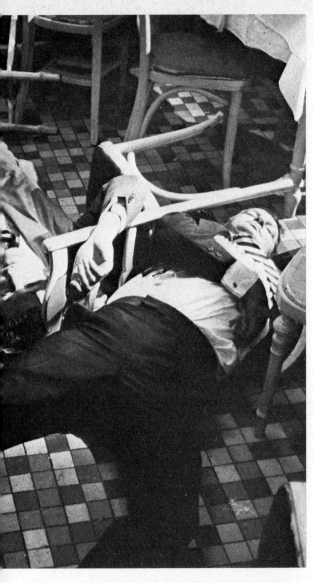

times to grind to a complete halt or, with the opening wedding-party, never to get started. And in a film which is in general very well acted, Marlon Brando's performance as Don Vito Corleone is the most grotesque among the reputed triumphs of screen acting since Vivien Leigh played Scarlett O'Hara.

The few other movies in the Mafia cycle are generally undistinguished: the films have little to offer apart from documentation, and that is mainly on the intricacies of the Mafia's family conventions rather than about what the Honoured Society actually does. Even this is blurred in Terence Young's atrocious version of *The Valachi Papers* (1972), in which a narrative of great clarity has been undermined by ham-handed compression, crummy staging and an assortment of dubbed supporting actors.

Even the frequently nimble Richard Fleischer did not manage to instil much life into the fictional narrative of *The Don Is Dead* (1973). The most satisfactory of Mafia movies to date is the most modestly budgeted of them, Paul Wendkos's film version of *Honor Thy Father* (1973). Apart from some ill-advised descents into the realms of slow motion and soft focus for occasional flashbacks, it manages to a greater extent than Fleischer's film to recapture some of the directness and economy that used to be among the virtues of even relatively undistinguished gangster movies. It would be interesting to know whether Bill Bonanno, who is sympathetically played by Joseph Bologna, would like it any more than he liked *The Brotherhood*. When he started a four-year prison sentence for a credit-card fraud on 18 January 1971, the Mafia movie cycle was only just about to begin.

diverse enough to include a contact man played by Benson Fong and has no visibly Italianate members should be referred to as the Mafia, almost as if the invocation of the magic word would help bring financial success (which was predictable anyway from chemistry of Matthau, Siegel and the story). In fact, after its false start with *The Brotherhood*, the Mafia boom in the cinema did not go very far beyond a single film, Francis Ford Coppola's embalming job on *The Godfather* (1971).

The unforgivable thing about *The Godfather* is the tedium. It is a film that has clearly been built to be an enormous success, the *Gone With The Wind* of the crime genre, which is to say a crime movie for people who despise crime movies but are impressed by gigantic, best-selling novels, a movie for people who do not even much like movies. Every bet seems to be hedged, even to the extent of avoiding the word Mafia to prevent offence to Italian Americans, and every character and event that the book's readers will want to be shown is faithfully produced, though the picture (perhaps not as a commercial proposition) would have benefited from a more ruthless hand on the structure to make the thing more of a movie and less of a waxwork show. The action is also so over-burdened with ethnic detail that it threatens at

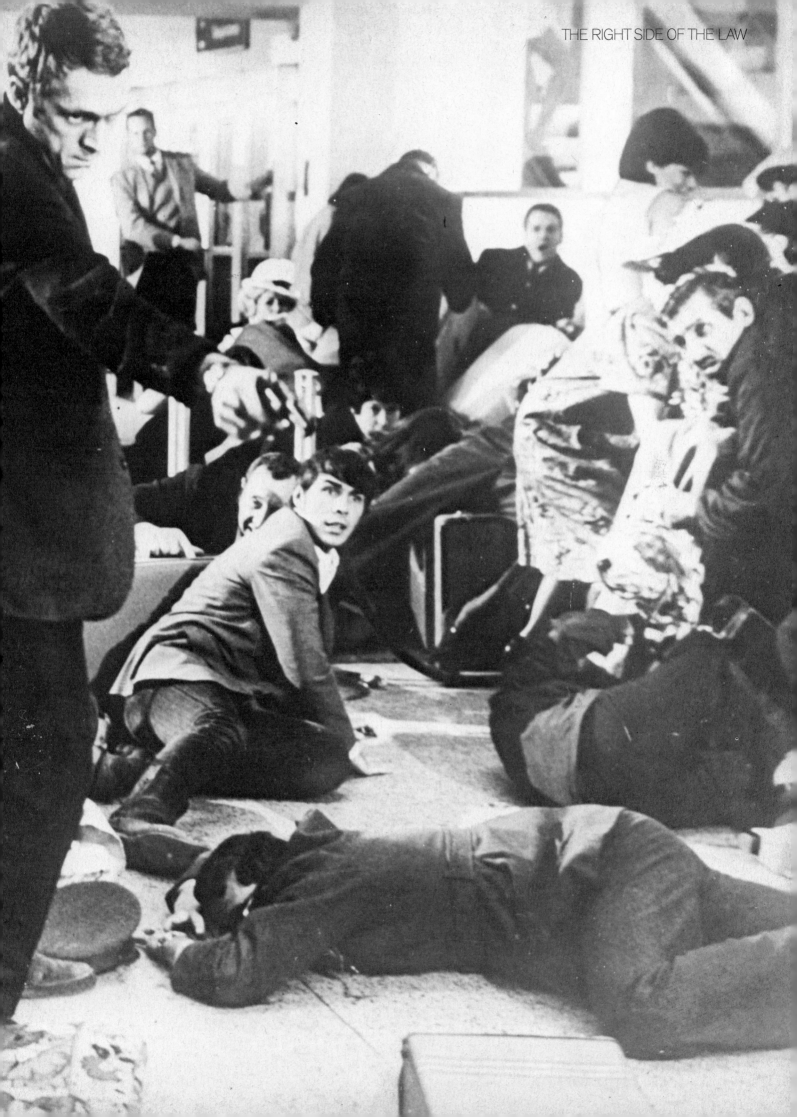

THE RIGHT SIDE OF THE LAW

'Your side of the fence is almost as dirty as mine,' Nick Bianco tells Assistant District Attorney Di Angelo in Henry Hathaway's *Kiss of Death* (1947). Bianco (Victor Mature) is reacting to a plan put forward by Di Angelo (Brian Donlevy) to conceal his new role as a squealer by planting the suspicion on one of his ex-partners. Di Angelo is quick to qualify Bianco's observation: 'with one big difference – we hurt bad people not good ones'.

Di Angelo is a stock figure of the period, the firm but enlightened representative of the law, confident and uncomplicated in his acceptance that law enforcement is a dirty business. Okay, one might imagine him saying, it may be a dirty business, but it has to be done. Such a straightforward attitude was not to survive for long, and as the problems became more fraught, the police and related professions developed into a much more interesting area for the movies, more interesting by far than the private eye.

This character, perhaps the most over-analysed in American fiction, had most of his finest hours in print and not on film, partly because the structure which embodies him does not lend itself to cinematic treatment. The difficulty has been summarised by Lawrence Alloway: 'There is an objective difficulty about presenting mystery on the screen: the absence of the criminal or doubt about his identity, entertaining in literary whodunits, has not thrived in movies. Gangster films and investigations of known criminals seem more amenable to physical enactment. The puzzle element was at a minimum in private eye films or at any rate was secondary to the present spectacle of luxurious apartments, sudden fights, ambiguous girls, and insomniac stress.'

Previous page: Steve McQueen in the final airport scene in *Bullitt. Right:* Robert Stack as Eliot Ness in *The Scarface Mob.*

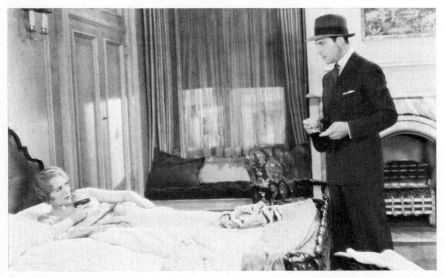

Humphrey Bogart, Peter Lorre, Mary Astor and Sydney Greenstreet in *The Maltese Falcon. Below:* an earlier version with Bebe Daniels directed by Roy Del Ruth in 1931.

The attractions of these films centre on such things and on the character of the investigator himself; the private-eye cycle makes a claim on the memory of most film-goers because the mystique which surrounds its supreme performer, Humphrey Bogart and two movies, John Huston's *The Maltese Falcon* (1941) from Dashiell Hammett with Bogart as Sam Spade, and above all Howard Hawks's *The Big Sleep* (1946) from Raymond Chandler with Bogart as Philip Marlowe. The crimes with which private eyes dealt were liable to be crimes of passion or plots so devilishly complicated and idiosyncratic as to have little in common with the more brutal concerns that have been explored in this book. Indeed, the puzzles which confronted private eyes often turned out not to be all that different from those solved, albeit with more genteel restraint, by their transatlantic counterparts, usually amateurs, in English detective stories.

It would not take too much of a wrench to transplant Hammett's Nick Charles, as impersonated by William Powell, together with Mrs Nick Charles (Myrna Loy) and the dog Asta into a British setting. In the series of six films which began with W.S. Van Dyke's *The Thin Man* (1934) and continued rather better with his *After the Thin Man* (1936), Nick Charles was a wealthy, amiable lush with a taste for low life exceeded only by his taste for cocktails expressed in such lines as 'Let's get something to eat – I'm thirsty.'

But Nick Charles was merely a gifted amateur and not to be confused with the less privileged

Victor Mature as Nick Bianco in *Kiss of Death*.

Humphrey Bogart, Lauren Bacall, Louis Jean Heydt and Sonia Darrin in *The Big Sleep*.

and specifically American persona of the shamus. His definitive form was Raymond Chandler's Philip Marlowe, whose transference to the screen by Howard Hawks with the help of three writers, William Faulkner, Leigh Brackett and Jules Furthman, is the one triumph of the cycle. (Not that the film is perfect – Max Steiner playing sorcerer's apprentice in the score sees to that – but perfection is not a particularly useful quality to look for in movies.) The magic, whether it was entirely calculated in advance or not, lies in the absolute congruence of the Marlowe character with Bogart's screen personality – that he was not infallible as an actor is demonstrated by, say, his performance as the Assistant DA in *Marked Woman* (1937); some of his later performances are also less than distinguished, but by this time he had learned to camouflage his limitations. Here Bogart never falters: every move, every inflection is exactly, instinctively right. The edgy tiredness that sums up a free-lance existence of perpetual instability is somehow transmuted into a component of the character's allure. Bogart manages this by embodying Marlowe's integrity, where other attempts at similar shamus figures have mainly captured their seediness.

It can only have been in the hope of re-creating the magic of Bogart in *The Big Sleep* that attempts have been made to revive in the 'sixties and 'seventies with other stars a form which was very much a phenomenon of the 'forties. Certainly, they could have derived little nostalgic inspiration from such other private-eye performances as Dick Powell in Edward Dmytryk's *Murder, My Sweet* (1945,

known in Britain under the title of the source novel by Raymond Chandler, *Farewell My Lovely*) or Mark Stevens in Henry Hathaway's *The Dark Corner* (1946). The late 'sixties brought a group of private-eye movies, of which the first and most successful is Jack Smight's *Harper* (1966, again known in Britain by the title of the original novel, *The Moving Target*, by Ross MacDonald). Even there, one has an uncomfortable feeling that the makers decided that since *The Big Sleep* the movies had grown up and that they ought to make a more 'adult' picture; the inclusion of drug addiction and torture hardly make up for the film's failure to do anything except stop dead as soon as it has manoeuvred its hero into confronting the problem of the nice guy (Arthur Hill) being the guilty party. Later 'sixties private-eye movies

Mary Astor and Humphrey Bogart in *The Maltese Falcon*.

175

William Powell and Myrna Loy in *The Thin Man*, and (*right*) in *After the Thin Man*.

have included Frank Sinatra in two directed by Gordon Douglas, *Tony Rome* (1967) and *The Lady in Cement* (1968), George Peppard in John Guillermin's *P.J.* (1968, called *A New Face in Hell* in Britain) and James Garner in Paul Bogart's *Marlowe* (1969). The most recent offerings in the field have been overtly retrospective: Roman Polanski's *Chinatown* (1974) is set in 1937, and Robert Altman's *The Long Goodbye* (1973), though set in the present, makes a point of how out of place Philip Marlowe, now played by Elliott Gould, looks in the present day.

The second really remarkable private-eye movie is Robert Aldrich's *Kiss Me, Deadly* (1955) which takes Mickey Spillane's thug hero, Mike Hammer, and, instead of keeping to the primitive morality of the author, uses

Hammer's brutishness (unflinchingly played by Ralph Meeker) to turn the film into a critique of Spillane. Aldrich also saw it as an anti-McCarthy picture: 'It was done at a time that you tried to say that the ends do not justify the means . . . it was an anti-Spillane picture about Spillane.'

There is a passage in Raymond Chandler's 'The Long Goodbye' that suggests that organised crime is, at least in the short term, an insoluble problem: 'We don't have mobs and crime syndicates and goon squads because we have crooked politicians and their stooges in the City Hall and the legislatures. Crime isn't a disease, it's a symptom. Cops are like a doctor that gives you an aspirin for a brain tumor, except a cop would rather cure it with a blackjack. We're a big rough rich wild people and crime is the price we pay for it, and organized crime is the price we pay for organization. We'll have it with us for a long time. Organized crime is just the dirty side of the sharp dollar.' It is perhaps through a similar, though less consciously formulated

Myrna Loy, William Powell and Joseph Calleia in *After the Thin Man*.

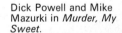
Lauren Bacall and Humphrey Bogart in *The Big Sleep*.

set of reasons that movies about cops and the like have, for all the optimistic finality of their conventional endings, become increasingly tortured in the years since the end of the Second World War.

In the pre-war days, the police in movies were largely untroubled by any of the more philosophical or spiritual questions that were to gather round the practical business of evening up the score on behalf of society. Confidence that they were the good guys often makes 'thirties cops now seem dislikeably smug. Lieutenant Flaherty (Thomas Jackson) in *Little Caesar* makes no secret of despising Rico: 'I'm your friend,' he sneers. 'I like to see a young fellow getting on in the world.' Flaherty realises that Rico's weakness is his pride and puts about suggestions belittling his former status and courage to winkle him out into the open for a final confrontation.

Success in the war against crime was measured by visible results: ethical hang-ups seemed irrelevant to a brand of law enforcement that could almost be judged by its body counts. Even in their titles, some of the 'thirties films suggest a cheery attitude that a dose of their own rough medicine would put the hoods out of business: *The Gang Buster* (1931), *Racket Busters* (1938), *Smashing the Rackets* (1939). All except the most red-necked of 'seventies audiences are likely to feel queasy about the message delivered by *'G' Men* that all the Feds

needed was the firepower to meet the underworld's violence on its own level. An FBI man gives a press conference urging the nation: 'Give your special agents machine guns, tear gas. . . .' What he wants to see is the Bureau's men 'equipped to shoot to kill with the least possible waste of bullets'.

In the following year, though, *Bullets or Ballots* did recognise a less clear-cut situation in which even cops could be corrupted and suggested the emotional stress of the undercover agent's position, an angle which was developed after the war, for instance in Joseph

Dick Powell and Mike Mazurki in *Murder, My Sweet*.

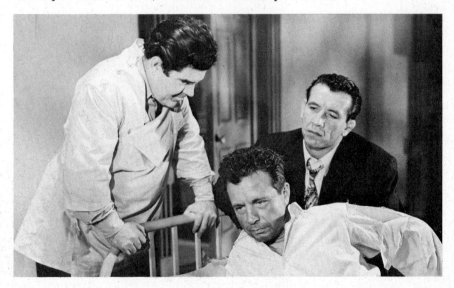

Lucille Ball and Mark Stevens in *The Dark Corner*.

Top right: James Garner and Gayle Hunnicutt in *Marlowe*.

George Peppard in *P.J.*
Right: Richard Roundtree in *Shaft*.

Before and after: Jack
Nicholson in Roman
Polanski's *Chinatown*.

180

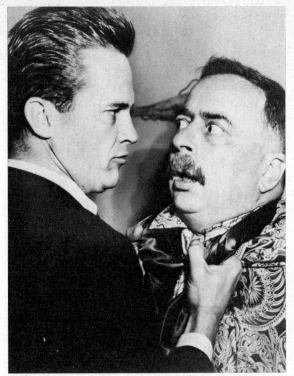

H. Lewis's *Undercover Man* (1949) and in *Loan Shark* (1952). But the presentation of law enforcement was not much modified or extended until after the war. The one image that became increasingly established was the enlightened lawman who was usually, like Di Angelo in *Kiss of Death*, behind a desk rather than out on the beat. But still, the officers of the law remained for the most part uncomplicated fellows just doing their jobs, and not even the most liberal of them, Di Angelo, ever lost sight of the fact that his job was to make sure that

punishment was meted out to the maximum number of bad guys.

One variety of post-war crime movie paid tribute to assorted forms of law enforcement, admiring the doggedness of the New York Police Department (*The Naked City*) or celebrating the work of some other Government agency, say, the Treasury (Anthony Mann's *T-Men*, 1947) or the Secret Service (*White Heat*) in much the way that war movies were often dedicated to the fighting unit whose exploits they depicted. This format kept going as late

'G' Men, with James Cagney and (right) Margaret Lindsay.

as 1959 and Mervyn LeRoy's lengthy tribute, *The FBI Story*, which included some words from J. Edgar Hoover himself and re-enactments of some of the reputedly glorious moments in that organisation's history, the deaths of John Dillinger and Baby Face Nelson and the wiping out of Ma Barker and her boys. The tribute format was invoked in all manner of films, including some with which it blends strangely – *Dirty Harry*, for instance, although there the tribute is not to the current law-enforcement scene but less controversially to the San Francisco police officers who gave their lives in the line of duty.

George Brent in Lloyd Bacon's *Racket Busters* (1938).

Edward G. Robinson reports to his superior after getting himself arrested in *Bullets or Ballots*.

Veronica Lake and her detective boy friend Robert Preston in *This Gun for Hire*.

183

The death of John Dillinger as depicted in *The FBI Story*.

Humphrey Bogart going back over the evidence in *The Enforcer*.

Even *The FBI Story* devotes quite a bit of footage to James Stewart's home life and his marital difficulties with Vera Miles who cannot come to terms with his devotion to the job. Quite apart from any professional or psychological problems that might come his way, the post-war cop often had to contend with an amount of flak on the domestic front. Even the most tolerant and stable of wives was likely to find at the very least that police life played hell with meal-times. Less complaisant wives were apt to show a degree of edginess about the hours, the risks and the bad pay. Much more than their husbands, the wives of dutiful cops gave voice to resentment at a society that undervalued its police and expected the cop to be, in Tom Flinn's words, 'an unlikely crusading knight whose services could be retained for $96.50 a week'. This background of conjugal discouragement extends right into the 'seventies, to Sidney Poitier in *They Call Me Mister Tibbs* and Stacy Keach in *The New Centurions* – Keach's wife actually leaves him. In a comedy, Jack Smight's *No Way To Treat a Lady* (1968), Detective Moe Brummell (George Segal) took a verbal pasting from his mother who didn't see what a nice Jewish boy was doing as a cop in New York.

The movies of the 'forties and 'fifties show increased evidence of the stresses bearing down on the police and the other representatives of the law. In life, these stresses could not have been new; what had changed was the emotional climate of the movies. Looking back today, not at particular films but at the movies of the 'thirties and 'forties *en masse*, one can sense a change, difficult to pin down, impossible to prove, towards a greater intensity or a greater degree of involvement on the part of the audience. A context which allowed even women's pictures and westerns to give their audiences a very much rougher ride than before could also accommodate similar developments in crime movies.

The main problem of the cops, apart from the danger and inconvenience and the low financial value placed on their services by the community, was enunciated by Humphrey Bogart in *The Enforcer*. The laws are designed to protect the innocent: what, then, do they do about guys they know are guilty? The penetration of criminal organisations by lawmen pretending to be crooks was an established, if stressful technique. Increased brutality was sometimes employed: Barry Fitzgerald's men in Rudolph Maté's *Union Station* (1950) obtain information from an unhelpful heavy by virtually waving him in the path of an oncoming railway train. The brutality is not necessarily physical. Before the credits of John Berry's *Tension* (1949), the detective from Homicide played by Barry Sullivan explains how you solve murders by piling on the tension until the guilty party cracks or does something to give himself away.

Lawmen could still be resilient and incorruptible like Di Angelo in *Kiss of Death* or the cop played by Stephen McNally in *Criss Cross*. Alongside them, though, were an increasing number whose behaviour was symptomatic of the stresses to which they were exposed. They were as fallible as other human beings. A District Attorney could be seduced by a scheming woman and thus become involved in covering up a murder case which he is supposed to be prosecuting (Robert Siodmak's *The File on Thelma Jordan*, 1949). Cops were liable to

Gene Tierney returns home from a weekend in the country in *Laura* to find Dana Andrews in her apartment investigating her apparent murder.

William Holden and Nancy Olson in *Union Station*.

185

Charles Bickford as the cop in *Fallen Angel* with (*above*) Linda Darnell as the girl he kills and (*right*) Dana Andrews and Percy Kilbright as two of the suspects he questions.

Dana Andrews covering up his accidental killing of a man he has been slapping around in *Where the Sidewalk Ends*.

behave no less oddly than other members of society: Dana Andrews as the detective in Otto Preminger's *Laura*, for example, falls in love with the girl whose apparent murder he is investigating. The brutal cop could use his interrogation techniques on the innocent as well as the guilty, even, like Charles Bickford in Otto Preminger's *Fallen Angel* (1945), to trying to pin on someone else the blame for a murder he had committed himself. A still more tortured treatment of related material occurs in a third Preminger movie, *Where the Sidewalk Ends* (1950), about a detective (Dana Andrews again) whose obsessive fight against criminals in general and Gary Merrill in particular has already got him into trouble with his superiors for the brutality of his methods. In slapping a murder suspect around, he accidentally kills

Joseph Wiseman and Kirk Douglas in *Detective Story*.

Evelyn Keyes and Van Heflin
with the body of her husband
in *The Prowler*.

Marla English and Edmond
O'Brien in *Shield for Murder*.

the man, a war veteran with a metal plate in his skull. As he has been unobserved, he tries to cover up by throwing the body into the river. The detective, still on the case, falls in love with his victim's wife. When the body is found, it is her father who seems to have the most motive and the least alibi for the killing. The detective pays for the best lawyer in town but eventually takes a more desperate way out: ' leaving a letter of confession, he goes out with the intention of getting himself killed by Merrill, so that at least his death will have

given the department something to pin on the hoodlum he most hates. Out of this ominous situation emerges a happy ending.

The cop as a neurotic was given a methodical working over in William Wyler's creaky film version of Sidney Kingsley's play *Detective Story* (1951), which traces Kirk Douglas's strong-arm methods back to his childhood traumas with a brutal father who drove his mother to insanity. The cop as neurotic shades into another figure who came up quite a number of times in the 'fifties: the cop as criminal.

Robert Stack as Eliot Ness with the Untouchables, including Keenan Wynn, Robert Osterloh and Paul Dubov in *The Scarface Mob*.

Jack Webb in *Dragnet*.

Touch of Evil. Right: Charlton Heston as Vargas tracking Orson Welles and Joseph Calleia with a radio receiver. *Opposite:* Orson Welles as Hank Quinlan, Janet Leigh as Vargas's American wife and Akim Tamiroff as Uncle Joe Grande.

In Joseph Losey's *The Prowler*, a police patrol-man (Van Heflin) uses his work as a cover for a scheme to murder his mistress's rich husband. This also relates back in pattern to the situation in a film like *Double Indemnity*. The motive in other crooked-cop movies was less entangled with sexual considerations: the lack of financial reward in police work motivated Steve Cochran and Howard Duff to robbery in *Private Hell 36* (1954) and Edmond O'Brien to murder as well in *Shield for Murder* (also 1954). In this film, which O'Brien co-directed with Howard W. Koch, he shoots a man he knows will be carrying $25,000 of underworld money, removes the bundle, yells 'Stop or I'll shoot', and fires in the air. Later he tells his protégé in the department 'Don't let it throw you kid – he was a crum.' It turns out that O'Brien has a record of rough-ness and an over-hasty shooting is not surprising from him. 'When are you going to stop thinking with your trigger finger, Nolan?' his superior asks him. When the young policeman discovers that he has also killed a deaf mute who witnessed the crime, O'Brien says that he has been living in dirt for sixteen years – some of it is bound to rub off.

One of the subsidiary concerns of the Syndicate movies of the 'fifties was the apathy of the public over the extent to which organised crime was corrupting their administrations and taking over their cities. In a position where their responsibility for dealing with crime from the ground up made the police a focus for bribes, intimidation, reprisals and assassination, as well as for pressures exerted from above by officers and officials whose integrity was under similar attack, the honest and un-

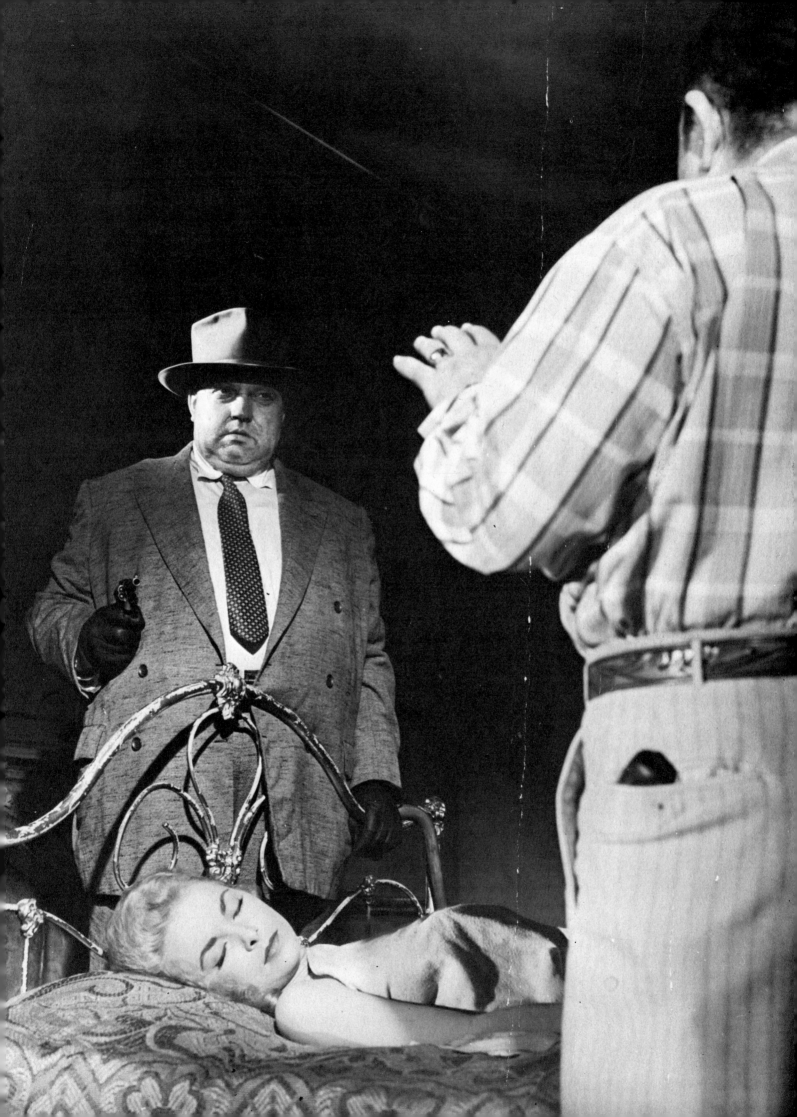

Scott Wilson, Rod Steiger and Sidney Poitier in *In the Heat of the Night*.

Marlon Brando beaten up by Richard Bradford and Clifton James in *The Chase*.

compromising cop was in an isolated and perilous predicament in which his successes were likely to be few and gained at great cost. It is easy to see that this situation could give rise to candidates for the role of avenging angel: obsessed, often psychopathic characters whose pursuit of justice (or usually revenge) did not accept any of the constraints imposed by the due process of law. It was as if these films, such as *The Big Heat*, had accepted the appallingly bleak premise that the normal resources of society were not equal to the task of cleansing and that only abnormal forces could do the job.

The late 'fifties and early 'sixties were something of a fallow period for cop movies: the weight of development in crime movies lay

with Robert Stack as Eliot Ness, the head of a squad of Prohibition-enforcing agents set up to be immune to the subversive attentions of the Capone gang. Lawmen are of course very much better central figures than criminals for television series: the same characters can be used in episode after episode. While the police were suffering an eclipse on the big screen, they were coming on very strong indeed in television, a much more conservative medium which exhibited a clean-limbed, mass-audience approach inherited from radio (an approach from which the cinema had been moving away since the late 'thirties, very slowly at first but gradually accelerating). Producing miracles of longevity hardly equalled in television outside the western and the daytime offerings of domestic sit-com, the police-story format has been a recipe so reliable that the succession of series continues unabated, even dominating the feature-length movies-for-television that have supplanted the old half-hour shows. The most notable of these recent products have been the series built round Peter Falk as Columbo and, particularly, Dennis Weaver as McLeod. Great ingenuity has been devoted to inventing similar formats built round related jobs: *Ironside*, crippled cop, was followed by

Sidney Poitier in *They Call Me Mister Tibbs*.

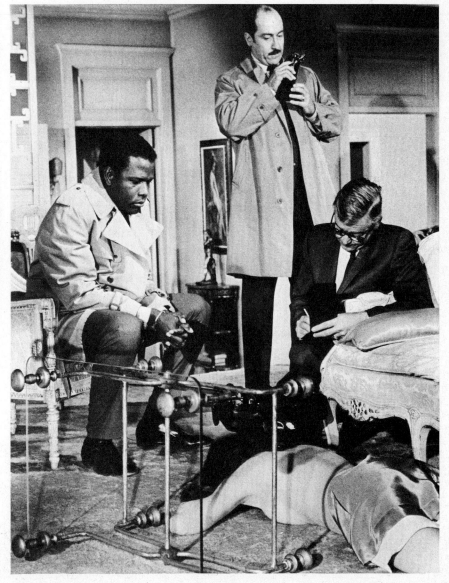

elsewhere. In the juvenile-delinquency cycle, the cop was frequently a peripheral and perhaps fatherly figure. The nostalgia cycle did not have much time for the police; the image of the 'twenties could be so much more strikingly put across, whether symbolically or sartorially, by concentrating on the hoods. In the first burst of nostalgic crime movies, only a couple of period films centred on a cop. Richard Wilson's *Pay or Die* (1960) was unique also in going back to before 1910; it is a biography of an Italian-born New York detective, Lieutenant Joe Petrosino (Ernest Borgnine), whose investigation of the Mafia was ended by his murder in Palermo in 1909. Phil Karlson's *The Scarface Mob* (1959) was made as the pilot for the Desilu television series *The Untouchables*,

Frank Sinatra in *The Detective*, with Lee Remick (*left*) and with Al Freeman Jr at the scene of the murder.

Longstreet, blind insurance investigator.

The most remarkable cop movie of the late 'fifties was undoubtedly *Touch of Evil* (1958) which came out of the interaction between a genre framework and a writer/director not accustomed to being tied down in that way. It is certainly Orson Welles's best movie since 1950 and arguably the most successful film he has made (not financially – the studio, Universal, hated it and released it with a marked lack of enthusiasm). It opens with an enormous travelling shot which starts with a time-bomb being placed in the back of a car and continues as the car is driven away, across the border from Mexico into the United States and through the border town until the bomb goes off. The killing is the start of the conflict between policemen from two sides of the border. Vargas (Charlton Heston) is efficient and sophisticated but Quinlan (Welles) is able to make a quick arrest by the simple expedient of framing the most likely suspect. He appears to have been using the technique for years, but before this he has usually fitted the frame round the guilty party. The climax of the film has a drunken Quinlan talking to his assistant (Joseph Calleia), who has reluctantly come round to Vargas's side and carries a radio transmitter, while Vargas tracks them at night with a receiver.

When the cop reappeared as a foreground figure in movies, his position had become a battleground for the opposing forces in American society. The first big success in the new cop cycle was *In the Heat of the Night* (1967) with a script by Stirling Silliphant (whose previous work had included *Nightfall* and *The Line Up*) and directed by Norman Jewison. This has a conflict that recalls *Touch of Evil*, but this time the primitive in the police force is a bigoted Sheriff in Sparta, Mississippi (Rod Steiger) and his sophisticated adversary is a black detective from Philadelphia who gets arrested for a murder and, being a homicide expert, solves the case and wins the Sheriff's admiration. Sidney Poitier later played the same character, Virgil Tibbs, in two more films, of which the first, Gordon Douglas's

195

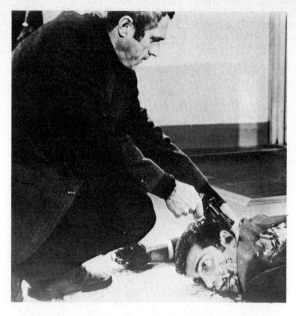

Steve McQueen gets his man in *Bullitt*.

The car chase in *Bullitt*.

They Call Me Mister Tibbs (1971) is notable for presenting him just as a detective, not as a black detective.

Contrasting with the carefully integrationist message of *In the Heat of the Night* and a follow-up, Ralph Nelson's *Tick . . . Tick . . . Tick* (1969) which puts Jim Brown as Sheriff into a southern town, was a strain of pessimism that had been most complete in Arthur Penn's *The Chase* (1966). The Sheriff of a small Texas town (Marlon Brando) is defeated by its violence and finally drawn into it. He survives a ferocious beating by a trio of town worthies and manages to arrest a man who has escaped from jail before would-be lynchers get to him (the details of a plot which has nearly twenty major characters are too complicated to recount here). Even then, the prisoner is shot on the steps of the jail by a man who has been present at the Sheriff's beating but not an active participant. The Sheriff sets upon the assassin with uncontrollable ferocity and has to be dragged off by his Deputies. Next morning he leaves town.

Richard Widmark in *Madigan*.

Robin Wood has noted the clear reference in the film of the killing of Lee Harvey Oswald but observes in it a more general implication: 'the sense that the traditional social values of western civilisation have been worn so thin that they are no longer capable of holding the forces that they have rendered the more explosive by suppressing'.

Some of the same pessimism, though more specifically directed at the breakdown in American urban society, informs Gordon Douglas's *The Detective* (1968), in which Frank Sinatra is a cop. In the earliest of a series of flashbacks, he tells his future wife that he is a cop because his old man was a cop, and *his* old man was a cop – 'it's the most useful thing I can be'. He attacks his colleagues, even physically, for their violence and corruption. He uses gentleness and persuasion to extract a confession of murder and gets a promotion that has previously eluded him because of his refusal to 'kiss ass'. But the man goes to the electric chair although he is visibly unbalanced. At the end, Sinatra is faced with the revelation that the man was innocent and that his own skill at his job has led to the execution: 'I knew that the poor bastard was a psychotic. He didn't know real from unreal.' Investigating the suspicious circumstances surrounding the

Harry Guardino and Richard Widmark come up against the killer (Steve Ihnat) whom they have been hunting in *Madigan*.

death of an accountant who was the real murderer, he also uncovers massive corruption among the members of the Borough Planning Commission who were 'selling land back and forth to make prices rise. By the time they've finished selling to each other, there isn't enough money to finance a bird house.' He is determined to expose this although he is told he will never win at trial – 'At least they'll know there was a contest.' But he turns in his badge to avoid hurting the department with his exposures – there are things to be done which he cannot do by being a cop.

The revival of cop movies which happened around 1968 might seem surprising in view of the mass of television cops. Most cop movies since 1968, though, have been very different from the television counterparts. They can, like *The Detective* and Don Siegel's *Madigan*, present a more uncompromising picture of police forces suffering from cowardice or opportunism at the top, brutality at the bottom,

Richard Widmark in *Madigan*.

197

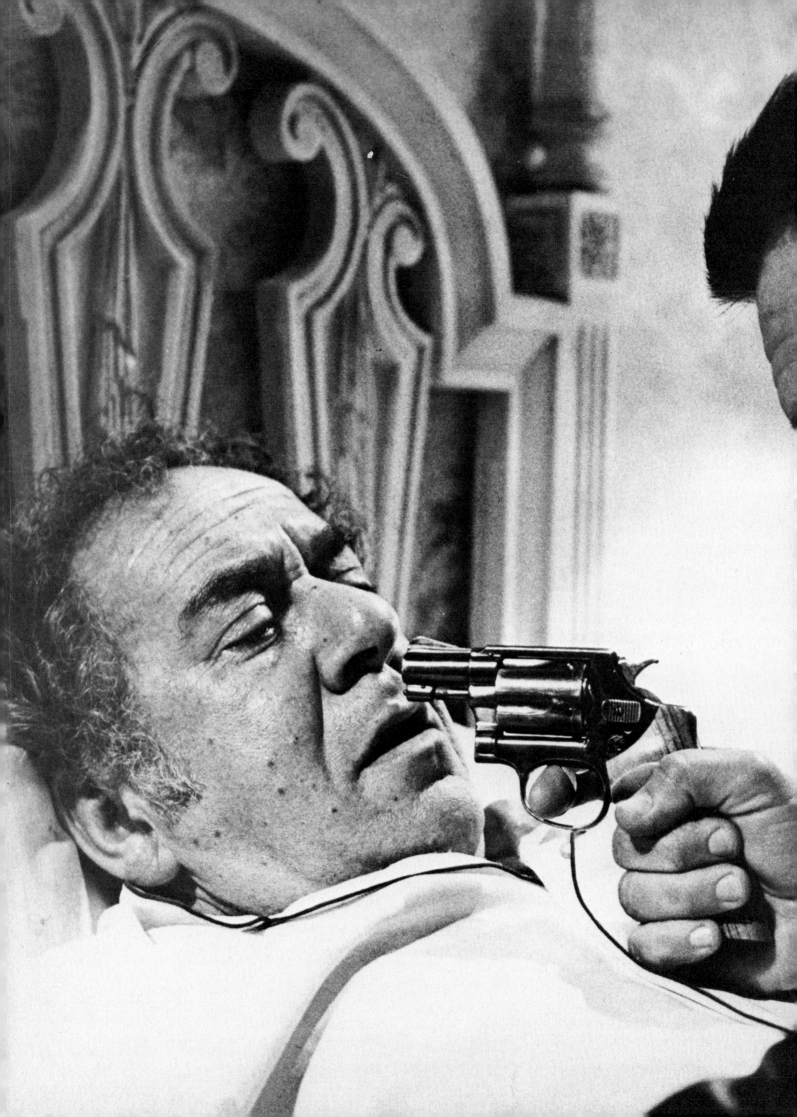

corruption and intolerance at any level. When a cop has shot someone in *The Detective*, Ralph Meeker says, 'Wait till those civil rights bastards get hold of this.' They can be more explicit in their violence and in other things: the opening scene of *The Detective* has Sinatra surveying the room which still has the naked body of the murder victim on the floor and mentions that the corpse has its penis cut off, the index finger and thumb of the right hand are missing and there are semen stains on the sheets. The cop is also allowed a freer life than television or previous movies offered him – this does not apply to Sinatra who cannot understand or forgive his wife's promiscuity, but is evident in another movie from the same year, Peter Yates's *Bullitt*, which has Steve McQueen provided with a girl friend rather than a wife. By the 'seventies, the sexual revolution has even got to John Wayne, the hero of John Sturges's *McQ* (1974).

Bullitt also displays another commodity that is not available to television crime efforts: money – the money for elaborate pieces of staging, which has unfortunately come to mean the car chases that are now part of the ritual in crime movies and often bring with them a degree of tedium in spite of the amount of destruction

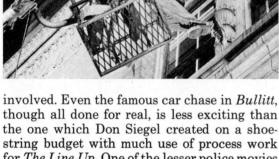

Top right: Clint Eastwood in *Coogan's Bluff. Above:* Clint Eastwood and Harry Guardino in *Dirty Harry;* Harry Callahan's superior watches him taping a flick-knife to his ankle, remarking that it is disgraceful that a police officer should know how to use such a weapon.

Clint Eastwood bringing down a man who has been contemplating suicide on a high ledge in *Dirty Harry.*

Robert Blake as John Wintergreen in *Electra Glide in Blue.*

but his attitude is not the product of a trauma but a reaction to the frame of reference within which he has to work. Harry reacts with vigour to situations as they present themselves and leaves the niceties to be sorted out later: 'When I see a man chasing a woman with intent to rape, I shoot the bastard. When I see a naked man chasing a woman through an alley with a butcher knife and he has a hard on, he's not out collecting for the Red Cross.'

More than any other recent crime movie, *Dirty Harry* stands as a document of its times, a presentation (albeit a pretty hard-nosed one using extreme circumstances) of problems which do not lend themselves to easy solution. The problem was defined exactly in an article by Clark Whelton on crime in New York's Sixth

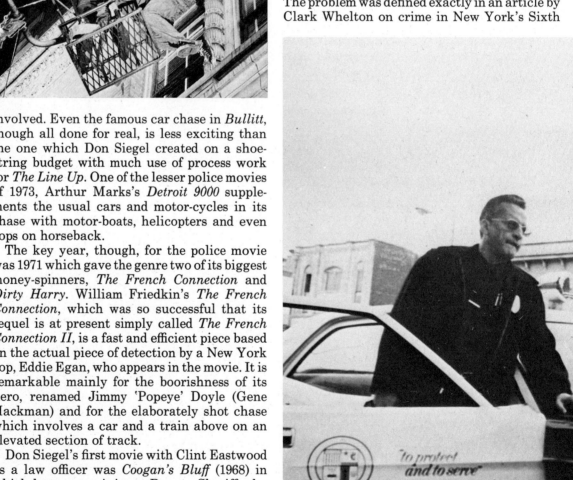

involved. Even the famous car chase in *Bullitt,* though all done for real, is less exciting than the one which Don Siegel created on a shoe-string budget with much use of process work for *The Line Up.* One of the lesser police movies of 1973, Arthur Marks's *Detroit 9000* supplements the usual cars and motor-cycles in its chase with motor-boats, helicopters and even cops on horseback.

The key year, though, for the police movie was 1971 which gave the genre two of its biggest money-spinners, *The French Connection* and *Dirty Harry.* William Friedkin's *The French Connection,* which was so successful that its sequel is at present simply called *The French Connection II,* is a fast and efficient piece based on the actual piece of detection by a New York cop, Eddie Egan, who appears in the movie. It is remarkable mainly for the boorishness of its hero, renamed Jimmy 'Popeye' Doyle (Gene Hackman) and for the elaborately shot chase which involves a car and a train above on an elevated section of track.

Don Siegel's first movie with Clint Eastwood as a law officer was *Coogan's Bluff* (1968) in which he was an Arizona Deputy Sheriff who loses a prisoner he is supposed to extradite from New York and finds himself out of his depth in the city. In *Dirty Harry,* however, Eastwood as Inspector Harry Callahan of the San Francisco Police is entirely at home in the city. He is as intolerant of the restrictions on his efforts as was Glenn Ford in *The Big Heat,*

Precinct which appeared in 'The Village Voice' of 13 September 1973. The police, it stated, 'are being asked to do a job which their fellow citizens don't want to do, and which they don't even want to *watch* being done. The police are being asked to function more and more like sanitation workers, taking care of our garbage in a way which neither involves us nor offends our sensibilities. Clean up the scum in Washington Square, but be nice about it. Clear the gay sado hustlers off West Street, but respect sexual preferences. Get the muggers and burglars off my block, but don't violate recent court rulings about loitering rules.'

Harry represents one reaction to occupying an exposed position in a society which appears indifferent, even hostile to his efforts. He becomes Superman, imperfect in his vulnerability to wounding by bullet and knife, sometimes fallible in his judgment, but as relentless and effective as human effort and skill can make him. Even then, he is frustrated – when he catches up with the killer (Andy Robinson), the only evidence is judged inadmissible, and the lad would not even be convicted of spitting on the sidewalk. Harry is ordered not to harass him when he is released. Seeing only what to him is the unacceptable face of liberalism, Harry consistently ignores the rules and

George C. Scott in *The New Centurions*.

orders which are likely to prevent him operating effectively. The problem which troubles Bogart's DA in *The Enforcer* twenty years earlier, the prosecution of the guilty with laws designed to protect the innocent, is more acute for Harry. Clark Whelton again: 'The limits of acceptable behaviour now border directly on the criminal. This change has worked in favor of virtually every minority and special interest group in the country, whose rights have been expanded and secured. It has also worked in favor of criminals, whose intentions are not equality but felony.'

George C. Scott and Stacy Keach in *The New Centurions*.

New Centurions (1972) that he has left himself no meaningful existence outside the police and shoots himself. Stacy Keach in the same film and Robert Blake in James William Guercio's *Electra Glide in Blue* (1973) are killed almost gratuitously – Blake is pursuing the hippily painted Volkswagen van only to give back a driving licence he has kept by mistake. Scott in *The New Centurions* embodies a grassroots response to law enforcement that is admirable in itself – a combination of alert sensitivity to the vibrations of the neighbourhood and a benignly empirical attitude to the law that is less concerned with rigid application of the rules than with finding the best possible solution to the immediate problem, whether it is getting a maltreated child away from its mother or going through the motions of rounding up the local whores and driving them around for a bit in the paddy-wagon before delivering them back in a state of happy inebriation. The cost is in the high calibre of personnel required and in the destructive effects of total immersion in a job that operates on moment-to-moment tension.

In the three years between *Dirty Harry* and *The Supercops*, the picture of the contemporary environment offered by cop movies has not become any more appetising. The policeman heroes who retain an image of their profession's nobility or even of its mystique are likely to be destroyed by it, like George C. Scott who discovers on retiring in Richard Fleischer's *The*

In the face of menaces ranging from organised crime to urban guerrillas, whose motivations he is unlikely even to understand, the cop may react with anything from ruthless pragmatism to wild paranoia. Richard Jordan as the Treasury agent in Peter Yates's *The Friends of Eddie Coyle* (1973) is armed with communications equipment of some sophistication – miniaturised earphones, and a microphone

Walter Matthau with Cathy Lee Crosby as the dead cop's girl friend in *The Laughing Policeman*.

taped to a finger – but relies ultimately on informers who are played for what they are worth in a way that is the complete negation of the scrupulous treatment accorded Victor Mature by Brian Donlevy in *Kiss of Death*. The agent has acquired the coldly professional characteristics of Syndicate killers in 'sixties movies; the extent to which he is untroubled by his job is caught in his use of a perfectly normal American piece of politeness at the end of each meeting with his informers: 'Have a nice day.' Paranoia is represented in a way that one fears is very much less of an enlargement than it seems by Mitchell Ryan as Harve Poole, the detective in *Electra Glide in Blue* who believes in the existence of a campaign of organised police genocide. He also has other problems which are announced by the drunken waitress who has been through the whole police force and compares him to the diminutive John Wintergreen (Robert Blake): 'I'll always like you, Harve, but I love Johnny. It's just that Johnny can do it three times in a morning, Harve, and you can't do it at all.'

There has hardly been a film since *Dirty Harry* which has allowed the police to retain even a vestige of its old image of top-to-bottom probity. Stuart Rosenberg's *The Laughing Policeman* (1974) and John Sturges's *McQ* (1974) are both old-fashioned detective stories which

McQ. Left: the confiscated drugs which should have been burned leave the hospital with the dirty linen. *Below:* Al Lettieri representing organised crime.

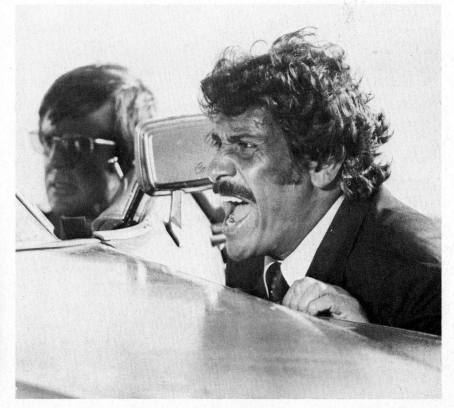

203

Joe Don Baker as Sheriff Buford Pusser at the end of *Walking Tall. Right:* his car bursts through the wall of the Lucky Spot Café.

Cop as executioner in *Magnum Force.*

display their modernity in the luridness of the garnish. *The Laughing Policeman* (known in Britain as *An Investigation of Murder*) almost submerges its story in details of police procedure and the San Francisco scene – Hell's Angels, drag queens, porno movie-houses, male go-go dancers – as if to grab at anything that might disguise its origins in a Swedish novel. When Walter Matthau's partner is among the passengers of a bus mown down by a machine-gun, Bruce Dern opines: 'Gotta be a hardcore crazy.' In fact, the dead cop had become obsessed with an unsolved murder, even to the extent of having his girl friend pose for pornographic photographs inspired by the case, and his killing was a job planned and carried out by the original murderer. The novelty of the crime lay in the machine-gunning of a busload of others, all except one of them (who had acted as a decoy) entirely innocent. *McQ* also starts with the killing of a policeman, which is put down to 'some radical getting it off'. But John Wayne discovers that the dead cop was involved in a narcotics racket, stealing drugs that were to be destroyed by the department. Worse still, Wayne has to leave the police and work on his own to reveal that a local official killed the cop and was planning to leave with his widow who is also involved in the drug business.

Meanwhile, hick-town police work is shown moving into an aggressive phase with Phil Karlson's *Walking Tall* (1973), a film 'suggested by certain incidents in the life of Sheriff Buford Pusser'. It also had a unique release pattern, starting with enormous success in the backwoods before emerging one year and many million dollars later in New York. On its home ground, the film's appeal was undeniable, with its hero going after the forces of sin and evil,

literally wielding a big stick. He starts as a private citizen confronting the mob by himself. Elected Sheriff, he moves the corrupt local judge out of his office and into the courthouse lavatory. Even shorn of twenty-five minutes for its British release, *Walking Tall* is pretty aggressive stuff, an expression of that old vigilante spirit. Almost two decades earlier, another small-town movie directed by Karlson, *The Phenix City Story*, had disturbed some critics by its violence. There, however, the lawyer returning home was shocked not just by Syndicate control of the town but by the

Clint Eastwood with two of the vigilante-minded rookie cops in *Magnum Force*.

205

citizens' response in forming themselves into vigilante squads. The end of *Walking Tall* has Pusser (Joe Don Baker) with his face covered in plaster – his lower jaw has been shattered by bullets – driving away from his wife's funeral to confront the two remaining heavies. He dispatches them by the simple expedient of ramming his car straight through the wall of their wayside gambling hell. He gets out with his big stick but there are no survivors. There is what amounts to a happy ending – the townspeople arrive in a horn-tooting motorcade, with the evident aim of backing their Sheriff up by lynching the bad guys. As they are too late, they drag out the contents of the Lucky Spot Café, pile them up and start a bonfire. On the soundtrack, the glutinous voice of Johnny Mathis sings a commercial for togetherness, telling us that we dare not wait and watch too long and that there's too much hatred all around. Sheriff Pusser, who acted as a consultant on the film (a traditional practice in true-story pictures) was on hand at press screening to vouch for the fact that what we see is 'about eighty per cent real'.

In a year which produced *Walking Tall*, it is not too surprising to find Inspector Harry Callahan surfacing again as the representative of a conservative approach to law enforcement. He may work, as his black partner tells him, 'close, real close', but he shows decent restraint compared to the younger cops who have formed themselves into an execution squad and are systematically wiping out the city's heavies. When Harry refuses to join them, they plant bombs in his and his partner's mailboxes. Harry defuses his bomb and goes on to discover that his rule-book superior (Hal Holbrook), who has been coming down on him for his violence, is the man behind the executioners. Harry contrives to kill the members of the squad and the Lieutenant.

The image of cops presented by the 'seventies law-enforcement cycle has been augmented by a new variety with some appeal to those who found the efforts of Harry Callahan or Buford Pusser ideologically antipathetic (however hypnotic they may have found them for other reasons). Sidney Lumet's *Serpico* and Gordon Parks's *The Supercops* both have heroes taken from life who are non-conformist in appearance and method in a way that is ultimately idealistic rather than authoritarian in intent. Frank Serpico and Detectives Greenberg and Hantz quiver with nervous energy when they are

pursuing criminals. They see the justification of their work as fighting crime and making arrests; anything that stops them has to be bad. Serpico finds himself up against a wall of police corruption, disliked for his appearance and for his steadfast refusal to take pay-offs. He finds that the only way to expose the corruption is to tell his story to the 'New York Times'. This works, but he is transferred to Narcotics and set up for assassination. He survives his injuries but leaves the force after testifying. He is said to be living 'somewhere in Switzerland'. Greenberg and Hantz also start as rookie cops in a film that offers a much more comic parallel to *Serpico*. Frustrated by the lack of opportunity to do what they reckon they are in the police for, they wade in and start making arrests on their own initiative in such quantity that they become known as Batman and Robin. The opening sequence of a presentation to the real Greenberg and Hantz records that they have been the subjects of assassination attempts and that they have made 600 arrests since they became patrolmen, mainly for gun and narcotic offences. Like Serpico, they come up against a police force permeated by corruption. Where Harry Callahan's methods are a reaction to the liberal niceties that he feels are hampering enforcement, they are driven to expedients often no less extreme because of the inadequacy of their colleagues to keep the law.

It is possible that the cop cycle is beginning to work itself out. The private detective does not seem to offer much new mileage except in a nostalgic context. The contemporary replacement could be the surveillance expert like Harry Caul (Gene Hackman) in Francis Ford Coppola's *The Conversation* (1974). The gambit of the bugger being drawn into the situation he is bugging offers obvious possibilities for development. On the other hand, the character is inherently sneaky and unattractive. The obsessive anonymity of Caul suggests kinship with another character, the professional hit man, like Claude in *Murder by Contract*. Perhaps he is destined similarly for intermittent exposure before taking his place in the gallery of crime-movie supporting parts. Although Coppola is said to have started the screenplay back in 1966, his film has clearly gained in public impact from the Watergate affair. An alternative protagonist who could emerge is the courageous investigative reporter, and even now Robert Redford is preparing to appear in a film based on the Bernstein and Woodward book 'All the President's Men'. But American audiences may be looking for a different, perhaps more comforting focus for their attentions. Prediction of this sort is always inadvisable for a form as closely affected as the crime movie is by current events. Even so, there could scarcely be a worse moment for prediction than now, shortly after the arrival of Mr Clean in the White House. With 'our long national nightmare' over and the relief as yet unbated, there is no telling where the concerns of the American public will encourage the cinema to explore.

POSTSCRIPT

This book has been confined to American crime movies to give it some chance of making meaningful generalisations. Only in America have crime movies been produced in sufficiently great quantity and with sufficient continuity to produce a developing genre that lends itself to being dealt with as such, though it can well be argued that crime movie is a portmanteau description covering a group of distinct but related genres. Outside America, however, one has to contend with occasional films or spasmodic bursts of interest in crime movies. One is then confronted with the dismaying prospect of being able to offer little more than a list with annotations.

The rest of the world, as far as crime-movie production is concerned, comes down largely to France and Britain, with lesser contributions from Germany, Italy and Japan. The relationship between the crime movies of these countries and the United States has almost entirely worked in one direction, with imitations of the American product. The exception to this rule was the pessimistic French crime movie of the late 'thirties, which seems to have had an effect on some Hollywood crime movies, particularly after the Second World War. Some of the films were also remade: Julien Duvivier's *Pepé-le-Moko* (1937) became John Cromwell's *Algiers* (1938); Marcel Carné's *Le Jour se lève* (1939) turned into Anatole Litvak's *The Long Night* (1947). But as a genre, the crime movie is almost as specifically American as the western, and even westerns have been made right across Europe from Almeria to Zagreb. On the old principle that one picture is worth a thousand words, the illustrations here have been chosen as a sample of the more interesting non-American crime movies.

Perhaps the best group of crime movies made outside the United States were those directed by Jean-Pierre Melville, including *Le Doulos* (*opposite*) with Jean-Paul Belmondo.

208

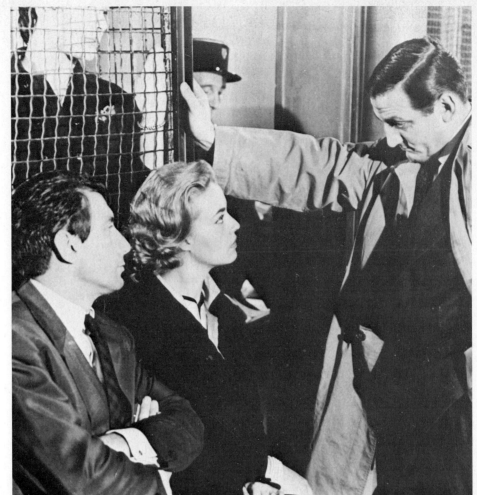

210

Far left: Jean Gabin in Jacques Becker's *Touchez-pas au grisbi* (1954) *Centre:* Jules Berry, Jean Gabin and Arletty in Marcel Carné's *Le Jour se lève* (1939). *Left:* Alain Delon in Jean-Pierre Melville's *Le Samourai* (*The Samurai*, 1967), playing a contract killer.

Right, top and bottom: Serge Reggiani in Jean-Pierre Melville's *Le Doulos*

A political fable which makes great use of American crime-movie imagery, Jean-Luc Godard's *Made in USA* (1966) with Anna Karina and Laszlo Szabo.

Centre and left: French crime movie made for export — Alain Delon, Jean Gabin and Lino Ventura in Henri Verneuil's *Le Clan des Siciliens* (*The Sicilian Clan*, 1969).

Symphonie pour un massacre (*The Corrupt*, 1963) directed by one of the more prolific makers of French crime movies, Jacques Deray.

213

Right: The French equivalent of the nostalgia cycle: Jean-Paul Belmondo and Alain Delon in Jacques Deray's *Borsalino* (1970).
Far right: Perhaps the natural mode for British crime movies, the backstreet squalor of Robert Hamer's *It Always Rains on Sunday* (1947) with John McCallum and Googie Withers.

George Nader in Seth Holt's *Nowhere to Go.*

Sam Wanamaker as the underworld boss in Joseph Losey's British film, *The Criminal* (1960).

214

Far left: British attempt at sleaziness: Tony Newley in Ken Hughes's *The Small World of Sammy Lee* (1963). *Left:* Gert Fröbe in Fritz Lang's *Die Tausend Augen des Dr Mabuse* (*The Thousand Eyes of Doctor Mabuse*, 1961).

German New Wave crime movie, Volker Schlöndorff's *Mord und Totschlag.*

ACKNOWLEDGMENTS

Where I have used descriptions or ideas from other writers, I have tried to quote directly rather than to paraphrase. The sources of such quotes are indicated in the text. I have also quoted without acknowledgment from previous articles and books which I have written.

I have used the following magazine sources: articles by V. F. Perkins and John M. Smith in 'Movie', by Tom Flinn (to whom I am also indebted for the Chandler quote) and Richard Whitehall in 'The Velvet Light Trap' and by Clark Whelton in 'The Village Voice'; interviews by Peter Bogdanovich, Stuart Byron and Martin Rubin in 'Movie'. My thanks to all these writers.

Among film books, I have been most stimulated by Lawrence Alloway's 'Violent America: The Movies 1946–1964'. I am grateful to Mr. Alloway for permission to quote at some length from his text. I must also thank the other authors and publishers whose books I have used. The following list includes the books from which I have quoted directly or indirectly.

Alloway, Lawrence: 'Violent America: The Movies 1946–64' (The Museum of Modern Art, New York, 1971).

Beman, Lamar T. (editor): 'Prohibition—Modification of the Volstead Law' (H.W. Wilson, New York, 1924).

Bogdanovich, Peter: 'Fritz Lang in America' (Studio Vista, London, 1967).

Cameron, Ian and Elisabeth: 'The Heavies' (Studio Vista, London, 1967).

Cameron, Ian and Elisabeth: 'Broads' (Studio Vista, London, 1969).

Chandler, Raymond: 'The Long Goodbye' (Houghton Mifflin Company, New York, 1953).

Furhammer, Leif and Isaksson, Folke: 'Politics and Film' (Studio Vista, London, 1971).

Gage, Nicholas (editor): 'Mafia, U.S.A.' (Playboy Press, New York, 1972).

Kitses, Jim: 'Horizons West' (Thames and Hudson, London, 1969).

Knight, Arthur: 'The Liveliest Art' (MacMillan, New York, 1957, copyright © 1957 Arthur Knight).

Messick, Hank and Goldblatt, Burt: 'Gangs and Gangsters' (Ballantine Books, a Division of Random House Inc., New York, 1974).

Messick, Hank and Goldblatt, Burt: 'The Mobs and the Mafia' (Thomas Y. Crowell, Inc., New York, 1972, copyright © 1972 by Hank Messick and Burt Goldblatt).

Talese, Guy: 'Honor Thy Father' (World Publishing Co., New York, 1971).

Turkus, Burton and Feder, Sid: 'Murder, Inc.' (Farrar, Straus and Giroux, New York, 1951).

von Sternberg, Josef: 'Fun in a Chinese Laundry' (MacMillan, New York, 1965; Secker and Warburg, London, 1966).

Wood, Robin: 'Arthur Penn' (Praeger, New York, 1970).

Illustrations
The stills used in this book come from the collections of John Kobal and the author, except for films in current release where stills have been provided by the distributors. Pictures are published by courtesy of their distributors and/or production companies: *distributors*: British Lion, Cinema International Corporation, Cinerama, Columbia-Warner, Fox-Rank, Gala, MGM-EMI, Miracle, Mondial, United Artists; *production companies*: Anglo-Amalgamated, Columbia, Ealing Studios, Filmel-CICC, Rob Houwer Film, MGM, Paramount, PRC, RKO, Rome-Paris Film, Twentieth Century-Fox, Universal, Warner Bros.

Opposite: spaghetti crime movie, *Gli Intoccabili* (literally, The Untouchables) with Britt Ekland and John Cassavetes.

INDEX

Figures in *italics* refer to
illustrations

Big Jim McLain

Boomerang

The Don is Dead

The Friends of Eddie Coyle

In the Heat of the Night

The Long Goodbye

The Man Who Knew Too Much

The Seven-Ups

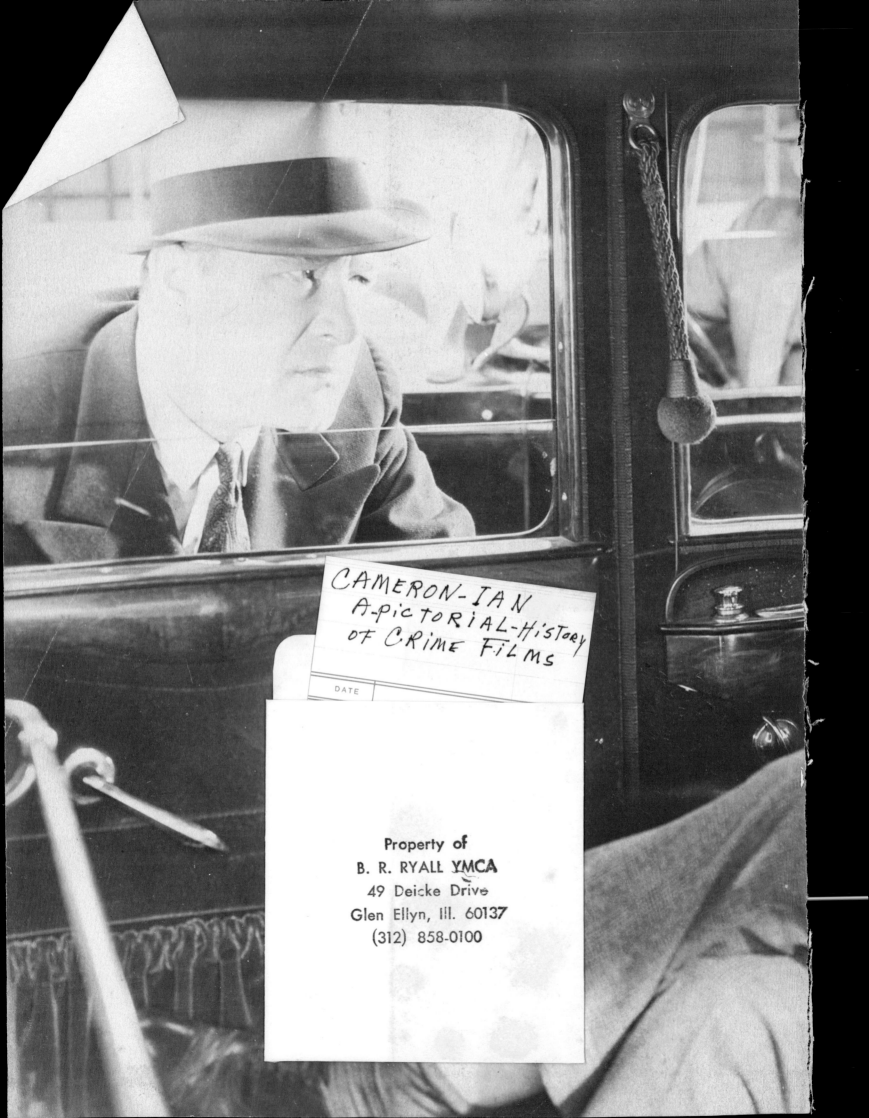

CAMERON-IAN
A-PICTORIAL-HISTORY
OF CRIME FILMS

DATE

Property of
B. R. RYALL YMCA
49 Deicke Drive
Glen Ellyn, Ill. 60137
(312) 858-0100